Julius Lloyd

Duty and Faith

An Essay on the Relation of Moral Philosophy to Christian Doctrine

Julius Lloyd

Duty and Faith
An Essay on the Relation of Moral Philosophy to Christian Doctrine

ISBN/EAN: 9783337078300

Printed in Europe, USA, Canada, Australia, Japan

Cover: Foto ©Thomas Meinert / pixelio.de

More available books at **www.hansebooks.com**

DUTY AND FAITH:

An Essay

ON THE RELATION OF MORAL PHILOSOPHY TO CHRISTIAN DOCTRINE.

BY

JULIUS LLOYD, M.A.,

RECTOR OF ST. ANNE'S, MANCHESTER,
AND ONE OF THE EXAMINING CHAPLAINS TO THE BISHOP.

JOHN HEYWOOD,
DEANSGATE AND RIDGEFIELD, MANCHESTER
AND 11, PATERNOSTER BUILDINGS,
LONDON.
1881.

CONTENTS.

CHAPTER VI —ALTRUISM.

CHAPTER VII.—UTILITARIANISM.

CHAPTER VIII.—EVOLUTION.

PART III.—RELIGIOUS PRINCIPLES.

CHAPTER IX.—THE CHRISTIAN DOCTRINE OF DUTY.

CHAPTER X.—THE CHRISTIAN DOCTRINE OF VIRTUE.

Chapter XI.—The Decalogue.

Chapter XII.—The Imitation of Christ.

DUTY AND FAITH.

PART I.

CHAPTER I.

INTRODUCTION.

MORAL PHILOSOPHY has for its subject no less than the whole of human conduct. In its full extent it comprises all the varied phenomena of action, affection, and desire. But in a more limited view, which is that of most practical treatises, Moral Philosophy deals mainly with two questions: (1) What is the standard of goodness in human actions? and (2) Why is every man obliged to conform to that standard? The former question suggests an inquiry into the nature of Virtue; the latter, into the nature of Duty. On these two ideas—Virtue and Duty—the whole of Moral Philosophy depends.

More briefly expressed: "What is right?" and "Why must I do right?" "right" being a quality of conduct which may be illustrated by such analogies as a line drawn straight, or a watch keeping true time.

These questions are evidently within the province of Christian Doctrine; and, in fact, several books exist in which the whole duty of man is deduced from the Bible. Nevertheless, Christian Doctrine is far from superseding the necessity of Moral Philosophy. For the precepts of Christ and the Apostles are for the most part incidental sayings, uttered with reference to special persons and special occasions, and leaving the application of the same principles to other persons in other circumstances to be inferred by reasoning, that is, by philosophical methods.

The use of reason in considering questions of right and wrong is implied, and even enjoined, in the New Testament. In several of the discourses of Christ, He reproves those who do not exercise their reason. "Why even of yourselves judge ye not what is right?" * "Are ye so without understanding?" † St. Paul speaks of Christian service as "reasonable," ‡ and describes his ministry as an appeal to the conscience of his hearers: "By manifestation of the truth commending ourselves to every man's conscience in the sight of God." § Without the recognition of such a faculty in man, all the internal evidence of the Christian faith, drawn from the moral beauty of Christ's teaching and the holiness of His example, would fall to the ground. To speak of God as wise and just would be unmeaning presumption on our part, if we had no faculty by which to discern wisdom and justice. But appeals to reason open a wide field, and cannot be satisfactorily made with exclusive reference to the Scriptures. Even in order to an intelligent appreciation of the plainest maxims of the Bible, it is necessary to survey the chief characteristics of Virtue and Duty as they are impressed by nature and habit on the conscience of mankind at large.

A scientific basis of morality, independent of Divine revelation, was sought in the study of Plato and Aristotle by theologians during the Middle Ages and since. New methods of inquiry have been opened by the progress of physical science. The discoveries of Newton and his contemporaries encouraged Locke to develop the philosophy of experience as applied to morals; and of late a fresh impulse has been given to these investigations by the observations of Darwin. The Evolution philosophy has thrown a light on the natural history of man, both in respect to his physical and his moral constitution, the effect of which it is premature to estimate.

So far as scientific principles can be determined they are to be accepted, in morals as freely as in medicine. We have already learned to recognise a scientific basis

---

* St. Luke xii., 57.   † St. Mark vii., 18.   ‡ Rom. xii., 1.   § 2 Cor. iv., 2

for some virtues, such as temperance and prudence. It is not from Scripture but from experience that men usually learn to abstain from unwholesome excesses, or to insure their lives. But there has been found no adequate basis for the higher order of social virtues, without appealing to the laws of the spiritual kingdom revealed in the New Testament.

The plan of the following essay is to examine, in the first place, the ideas of Virtue and Duty in their general form, and to consider whether the intuitive faculty of conscience, or moral sense, which is common to the world at large, is sufficient of itself to dispense with the philosophical study of right and wrong; then, in Part II., to examine the four principles which underlie the philosophical treatment of the subject; namely—Egoism, the principle which has its centre in self: Altruism, which excludes self-regard in care for others: Utilitarianism, which measures human happiness impartially, without selfish or unselfish prepossession: and Evolution, which rises to a more comprehensive view, treating human life as a portion of the phenomena of the universe. Lastly, in Part III., I shall try to show the connexion between Christian Doctrine and the elementary ideas of Duty and Virtue, with more particular reference to the Moral Law of the Decalogue, and to the character of Christ as an example.

CHAPTER II.

THE IDEA OF VIRTUE.

Both in Greek and Latin the word which is equivalent to Virtue means, properly, manliness. This use of terms is illustrative, not only of the original idea, but of the essential character of Virtue in general, as distinguished from the special properties which are called virtues. It denotes the perfection of human nature as a whole; a type of goodness, complete according to an ideal conception of that which man is at his best. The word in its full significance is not restricted to masculine qualities. What it implies is a combination of good elements, and that not casual or momentary, but deliberate and habitual,* so as to cover all the various offices of human life.

A celebrated statue by Polycletus, representing a soldier armed with a spear, was called by Greek artists the Canon, or Rule, as being a model of beautiful proportion. To discover such a normal standard of right conduct is the task which we have before us, if we attempt to define the idea of Virtue. It is not enough to draw up a catalogue of particular virtues to be embodied in a perfect man, and of particular vices to be excluded, but to show the several elements of manhood in due proportion and symmetry, like the features of a countenance, or the form of a well-grown body. Merely to say that Virtue is composed of courage, temperance, justice, &c., is no more than to say that a face is composed of eyes, nose, and mouth. The form of each remains to be described, and its relation to the rest.

Another suggestive comparison is given by Plato in a passage quoted from Simonides: "It is hard to become truly a good man, four-square in hands and feet and mind, fashioned without fault."†

The word "four-square" conveys vividly two characteristics of the idea of Virtue, namely completeness and rectitude. It is used in this sense with much felicity in Tennyson's "Ode on the Death of the Duke of Wellington":—

> O fall'n at length that tower of strength
> Which stood four-square to all the winds that blew !

From the conception of Virtue as quadrilateral has arisen the fourfold division which is recognised by ancient and modern moralists, of the four cardinal

---

* Aristotle, "Eth. Nic.," ii.　† "Protagoras," xxvi.

virtues: Wisdom, Justice, Fortitude, and Temperance, a scheme which is thus expounded by Cicero :—

All that is honourable springs from one of four divisions. Either it has to do with perception of truth and intelligence; or with the defence of human society, in giving to every one his own and keeping faith ; or with magnanimity and invincible courage ; or with the order and measure of that which is done or said, in which moderation and temperance consist.[*]

But the abstract idea of Virtue involves another element, which is in some measure at variance with statuesque completeness. The relation of each individual man to his fellow-men is a condition of goodness, which tends at every moment to modify the rule of Virtue. He is a son, a brother or husband, a citizen, a master or a servant or not improbably both; and these various relations must be taken into account. Virtue is, above all things, a rule of practical conduct.[†] Hence the inquiry as to what is good for a man's self is inseparable from an inquiry as to what is good in relation to others. To be good, without doing good, is a state which may be imagined as possible for some other order of beings, but not for man. The question arises whether, and in what sense, we are under an obligation to do good, apart from the preference for Virtue which we may entertain of our own voluntary choice.

CHAPTER III.

THE IDEA OF DUTY.

WITHOUT a sense of Duty, Virtue would be little more than a branch of social culture: a sort of fine art, or department of " the Beautiful," as it seems to have been held in the philosophical period of Greece. The idea of Duty is that which gives to moral precepts an imperative authority, binding upon the conscience. In the idea of

---

* " De Officiis," v.   † "Virtutis laus omnis in actione consistit."—*Ibid*, i., 6

Virtue, apart from Duty, there is not of necessity a religious element; but Duty is properly and essentially religious. However its nature and origin may be defined, a characteristic of Duty is sacredness; and to those who have regarded popular forms of religion with little sympathy, a strong sense of Duty has often been a sort of religion in itself. So it was to Socrates, who personified Duty as a familiar spirit who taught him what to do, and what not to do.* So it was no less to the great Roman philosophers, Cicero, Seneca, and Marcus Aurelius. The exact measure of their faith in the deities of Rome is doubtful; but it may be certainly affirmed that their deepest and most religious devotion was paid to the law of conscience within, above all popular religion.

The word Duty is of Latin origin, and properly means a debt. Associated with Duty is the word obligation, which implies a necessity that the debt must be paid; for the sense of *obligatio*, as a technical term of Roman law, is defined in the Institutes of Justinian to be a legal bond for securing payment. In English the word "ought" has a similar derivation, being a disused tense of the verb "to owe." The philosophical use of these terms is to some extent figurative; and one of the most difficult problems of moral philosophy is to determine how far the legal metaphor which they suggest corresponds with fact: how far moral obligation is a reality, and what is its true obligatory force. When an action is called a duty, it is implied that the action must be done under constraint, if not willingly; that severe penalties of some kind follow on leaving it undone. In this respect Virtue and Duty are contrasted ideas. Virtue is free, and much of its excellence consists in freedom; but Duty holds us bound by an invisible moral chain, which operates on our souls, like gravitation upon the planets.

A manifest and intimate connection subsists between Duty and Law. If the law of the land represents fairly

---

Xenophon, "Memorabilia," i., 2.

the supreme law of the universe, no further definition of Duty need be sought than obedience to law. A good man, according to Roman ideas, was "one who keeps the decrees of the fathers, the laws and ordinances." In modern times, however, the province of positive law is more restricted, and the conception of a higher law has been developed in various forms. According to one school of moralists, Duty is allegiance to a Law of Nature, which can be inferred from the order of nature in general, or of human nature in particular. Our conscience is the exponent of such a supreme law. It is in this manner that Bishop Butler treats the subject:—

Allowing that mankind hath the rule of right within himself, yet it may be asked, "What obligations are we under to attend to and follow it?" I answer: It has been proved that man by his nature is a law to himself; without the particular distinct consideration of the positive sanctions of that law; the rewards and punishments which we feel, and those which from the light of reason we have ground to believe, are annexed to it. The question then carries its own answer with it. Your obligation to obey this law is its being the law of your nature. That your conscience approves of and attests to such a course of action, is of itself alone an obligation.*

There are several ambiguous terms in this theory of moral obligation, which have led moralists of a different school to understand obligation in a less abstract sense. For instance, Paley says, "A man is said to be obliged, when he is urged by a violent motive, resulting from the command of another;" and he applies this definition to the question, "Why am I obliged to keep my word?" by answering, "because I am urged to do so by a violent motive (namely, the expectation of being after this life rewarded if I do, or punished for it if I do not), resulting from the command of another (namely, of God)."†

Between these two views of the nature of obligation the opposition is more on the surface than in substance If the approval of our conscience is of itself an obligation, that is not presumably because of any original or supreme authority inherent in our conscience, but rather because our conscience is the interpreter of a

---

* Sermon III., "On Human Nature." Works, ii., 32.
† "Principles of Moral and Political Philosophy," book ii., ch. v., vi.

Divine law, which has in reserve the rewards and punishments of a future life. Nevertheless, while the two theories admit of reconciliation, the aspect which they present is widely divergent. The idea of Duty alters its appearance to our minds according as we connect it with simple reverence for law or with the consideration of private advantage. To do our duty for reward, whether in the present life or in the life to come, is certainly not the purest way of doing our duty. There is much that commands our respect, if not our unqualified assent, in the other theory that Duty, as dictated by our conscience, carries its own adequate sanctions, requiring no appeal to ulterior consequences; that the word "you ought" sufficiently conveys the meaning "you must," without urging the penalties of disobedience. But our adoption of the dictates of conscience as a Divine law will depend on the measure of certainty which we can ascribe to the moral intuition of conscience.

CHAPTER IV.

MORAL INTUITION.

By Moral Intuition is meant the faculty which is sometimes called a moral sense, the faculty of judging between good and evil in human actions by simple discernment, as we judge of colours, without giving or seeking a reason.

That we have such a faculty is proved by familiar experience. Its existence and power are demonstrated by the successful appeals to it which are made by orators. If Cicero denounces the effrontery and guilt of Catiline; if Burke inveighs against Warren Hastings as the common enemy and oppressor of the human race; if Curran pleads that emancipation of the slave is the immediate result of touching the sacred soil of Britain, these and similar efforts of oratory are addressed to a faculty of moral judgment which acts with intuitive readiness. The question to be considered in relation to this faculty is, how far it is a sure or sufficient guide as to our conduct.

Any one who has attended a trial in which the pleas of justice and mercy are urged on opposite sides, will be aware that the intuitive judgment of the hearers is apt to waver, as one consideration or the other is brought into prominence. This is not only in consequence of new facts which may be elicited as the case proceeds, but depends on the point of view from which the facts are presented by the advocate. In Shakspere's play of "Julius Cæsar," we have an admirable illustration of such alternating moral sentiments. Brutus is represented as justifying his share in the death of Cæsar, as an act of self-devotion to the liberties of Rome :—

"Not that I loved Cæsar less, but that I loved Rome more."

"Who is here so base that would be a bondman ?
If any, speak; for him have I offended."

"Who is here so vile that will not love his country ?
If any, speak ; for him have I offended."

Presently Mark Antony, in a speech full of subtle insinuation, moves the hearts of his audience in Cæsar's favour.

"He was my friend, faithful and just to me."

"When that the poor have cried, Cæsar hath wept."

"You all did love him once, not without cause."

Each point in either appeal touches a sympathetic nerve in the hearer's conscience : on the one side, liberty and patriotism ; on the other side, friendship, gratitude, compassion, the memory of Cæsar's great deeds, the treachery of the friend whom he had trusted, "for Brutus, as you know, was Cæsar's angel." These are examples of the various elements which go to form our decision as to character and conduct in any disputed case; and a moral intuition which is hasty and ill-informed is apt to shift to and fro, like the citizens in the play. Similarly in a great political crisis, when party spirit runs high, friends and members of the same family are drawn to opposite sides by conflicting moral sentiments: not that they differ as to abstract principles of virtue, but as to the relative magnitude of duties which cannot be reconciled in the particular instance.

A few general principles are affirmed with one consent by the universal voice of civilised mankind. Bishop Butler says:—

Much as it has been disputed wherein virtue consists, or whatever ground for doubt there may be about particulars, yet in general there is an universally acknowledged standard of it. It is that which all ages and all countries have made profession of in public ; it is that which every man you meet puts on the show of; it is that which the primary and fundamental laws of all civil constitutions over the face of the earth make it their business and endeavour to enforce the practice of upon mankind : namely, justice, veracity, and regard to common good.*

Probably it is true, as a recent writer states, that " no moralist denies that cruelty, falsehood, and intemperance are vicious, or that mercy, truth, and temperance are virtuous."†

Nevertheless, when the general idea of Virtue is analysed, and the several parts compared, this unanimity ceases. All men approve of Justice in the abstract; but philosophical treatises without number have been written to describe the nature of Justice as to its elementary principles, and able writers are at issue on such fundamental questions as whether private property in land is just. All men likewise approve in the abstract of Veracity and regard to the common good; but a critical question arises whenever Veracity is thought to be an obstacle to the common good. Macchiavelli's treatise, " The Prince," is notorious for a deliberate advocacy of deceit in politics. It appears, therefore, that Moral Intuition is an uncertain guide, not only as to particular cases, but as to general prin-

---

* Works, vol. i., p. 313.
† L. Stephen's "Science of Ethics," p. 1.

ciples, as soon as they are drawn out with sufficient precision to be applicable to practice.

The cardinal virtues of the ancients are approved by the conscience of mankind, at least in comparison with the opposite qualities; that is, wisdom is preferred to folly, justice to injustice, fortitude to cowardice, temperance to intemperance. But in practical questions of conduct these virtues do not come before us singly for approval. They mingle together in various proportions; and other virtues, such as benevolence, humility, purity, enter into the character and conduct which our conscience approves.

Various distinct types of character are formed, according as one or other of these elements may predominate, and no exercise of the faculty of Moral Intuition is more important than the selection of a favourite type. The question, What is right? is commonly answered by a typical example, rather than by an abstract definition, in the ordinary conduct of life. Such types are impressed on the consciences of individual men, sometimes by private study, but more often by the influence of the spirit of the age in which they live. At certain periods, and in certain social conditions, the ideal of manhood has been military, and the virtue of courage has been magnified out of its true proportion. Under altered circumstances virtues of a different class—philosophical, ascetic, or domestic—have been exalted in their turn. As each phase of life passes out of fashion, the imperfection of its ideal becomes manifest, though unobserved before. A few prominent examples will serve to illustrate the variety and the potency of this kind of moral forces.

Of the Heroic type, there is no more adequate specimen than the Homeric Achilles. His incomparable excellence in all martial exercises, his terrible war-cry and headlong valour, his swiftness of foot, his beauty of face and form, his passionate impulses of love and anger, present an image complete after its kind of manhood, according to the popular ideal of the age to which it belongs. How deeply this type, with all its characteristics, was imprinted on the minds of later generations in Greece, is

2

shown by the savage conduct of Alexander, when he
dragged the defender of Tyre behind his chariot, in
imitation of Achilles dragging the body of Hector. And
still, wherever Greek culture has penetrated, this heroic
type retains something of its attractiveness, especially
for boys.

A second type of character, the Philosophic, is well
represented by Socrates, as he appears in the writings
both of Plato and Xenophon. A mind intent on truth
and righteousness, in obedience to the dictates of a voice
within, missionary zeal to expose ignorance and shallow
pretension, fearless integrity, callous indifference to the
pleasures and pains of mortal life, with no less indifference to purity of morals, are parts of a consistent whole,
in which the several elements so combine that he stands
forth in literature as the ideal type of a seeker after
knowledge, an inquiring Agnostic.

A third type of character, the Patriotic, is abundantly
illustrated in the history of many nations, most of all,
perhaps, in that of Rome. Fabricius treating with scorn
the gold and the elephants of Pyrrhus, Regulus dissuad-
ing his fellow countrymen from peace with Carthage,
and choosing rather to go back to captivity and torture,
are notable among less familiar examples.* But the
idea of patriotism, from its very nature, tends to sink
the greatness of the individual in that of the commonwealth; so that Roman history, as a whole, breathes a
spirit of patriotism more intense than the biography of
any single Roman. The patriotic type of character, of
which our own day has seen a winning example in
Garibaldi, derives much of its fascination from self-
effacement in disinterested ardour for a national cause.

Christianity has produced special types of character
unknown to the ancient world. Among these is hardly to
be reckoned the ascetic type in its sterner forms, as exhibited in the hermits of the Nubian desert; for these have
their counterpart, and perhaps their origin, in the devotees
of the far East. There is, however, a milder type of

---

* See Cicero, "De Off.," iii., 26, and Augustine, "De Civ. Dei.," i., 15.

Asceticism which is essentially Christian, being associated with purity, humility, and charity. If one name
is to be selected as an ideal representative of this type,
the choice might well fall upon a woman, and that
woman St. Elizabeth of Hungary. The stones of her
memorial chapel at Marburg, worn by the knees of
pilgrims, bear testimony to the reverence kindled by
her self-devoted life, in which the love of God and her
neighbour became an enthusiasm of sacrifice too exacting
for human infirmity to support.* Her virtues are commemorated in numerous mediæval pictures, in which she
is represented as tending the loathsome sores of the
poor, or bearing in her robe the miraculous roses which
attested the Divine approval of her almsdeeds.

Comparing together examples such as these, each of
which illustrates a moral standard of immense and enduring influence on human conduct, it is evident that
the faculty of Moral Intuition is far from uniform in its
approbation or disapprobation. What is in harmony
with the highest virtue, according to one standard,
is ignored, despised, or even condemned as vicious,
according to another. There is on several points an
apparent antagonism between Christian meekness and
heroic magnanimity, between Christian faith and Socratic
doubt, between national patriotism and the universal
citizenship of the Kingdom of Christ.

A comprehensive philosophy reconciles these and other
conflicting sentiments, by assigning to each its proper
limitation, but they are not to be reconciled by any
merely intuitive process. In fact, the diversity of Moral
Intuition in such questions is a fruitful cause of party
strife between men who are loyal on either side to the
dictates of their conscience. Now, this diversity points
to two alternatives. Either there is no permanent standard of right, or else the faculty of Moral Intuition is not
sufficient, unaided, to determine what is right.

If the former alternative be taken, and "right" be used
as relative only to the variable standard of our own

---

* See Montalembert, " Vie de St. Elisabeth."

conscience, we are brought quickly to a result which is
self-contradictory. A man will say, "I was wrong" if
his mind has changed; "I intended to do right, but I
see my error now." In such a case the judgment of his
conscience must be at fault, either in his former approval
or in his present recantation. If whatever seems right
is right, a man is wrong to blame himself for doing
what seemed right; that is, he is at the same time
both right and wrong—right on the supposition that
his conscience is its own rule, wrong in allowing himself to doubt the sufficiency of that rule. Whether the
standard of right be absolute or dependent on circumstances, it is at all events universally recognised as being
more permanent than the variable moods of each man's
conscience. That seeming right and being right are
identical in moral conduct, is a proposition which hardly
bears discussion.

We are compelled therefore to look beyond mere
intuition for some criterion of right. Yet while we
conclude, as we must, that the faculty of moral intuition is insufficient to determine what is right, we are
nevertheless constantly dependent on our moral intuition for guidance in the affairs of common life, and
also for help in discovering the criterion by which our
conduct can be regulated more certainly. The Supreme
Rule of human action, that is, in other words, the ideal
standard by which right and wrong are measured,* can
only be recognised as such by the exercise of our faculty
of moral intuition, and can only be applied to practice
by the exercise of the same faculty. Practical conduct
must in any case be governed by the exercise of a
moral judgment which works so spontaneously that it
is not inappropriately termed a moral sense; and speculative theories, however plausible intellectually, must
stand or fall by the test of their conformity to the moral
sense of mankind.

For the power of discerning right from wrong is not
merely an intellectual faculty. If it were so, the word

---

* Whewell, "Elements of Morality," Art. 73.

"right" would be as emotionless a term as the geometrical term " straight;" and wrong would mean simply crooked. A wrong action would differ from a right action only as an oak differs from a poplar, or a bow from an arrow. All that is sacred in moral rectitude belongs to a faculty distinct from intellectual perception, a faculty which in popular language bears the name of conscience; and the province of moral philosophy is not to supersede the intuition of conscience, but to develop, inform, and correct it.

Conscience has a twofold operation—intuitive and reflective. One part consists in approval or disapproval of actions in general as right or wrong; the other part consists in applying these general rules to our own case personally. This distinction is illustrated by cases in which, as in the well-known instance of David, a man pronounces a severe condemnation of an action of his own unawares, and experiences a second and distinct emotion on being reminded that the deed was his.

There is a close analogy in several respects between the moral faculty of conscience and the faculty of sight. Most of the imperfections of our visual organs have their counterparts in our Moral Intuition. Near sight and far sight, the latter being the tendency of advancing years, correspond to the mental habits of the imprudent and prudent respectively. The effect on the eye of sudden change, from darkness to light or from light to darkness, corresponds to the bewilderment of moral sense which is experienced by travellers, when they come on a sudden among people whose code of right and wrong is unfamiliar. In such cases it is not long before conscience, like the eye, adapts itself to its new environment. Another imperfection of the eye is that it has no natural sense of perspective, and is slow to acquire by practice a knowledge of the real size of distant objects. To this corresponds the ignorant prejudice which disables a child or a savage from taking a right measure of relative duties. Nevertheless, in spite of these and other defects, the eye is the organ by which we see whatever we can see. No optical instrument can do more than facilitate the exercise of a faculty of sight given by nature. And similarly, the speculative principles of moral philosophy, by which our conscience is guided, presuppose the action of our conscience. Moral systems to a man without a conscience would be as glasses to the blind. Definitions of right and wrong, however just, are ineffectual to the mind which has no true sense of moral distinctions. For instance, no demonstration that falsehood and cowardice are unreasonable would touch that chord in human nature which thrills with indignant emotion at the sound of the words "liar" and "coward." So, throughout the whole compass of moral philosophy, the primary intuitions of conscience have their distinct office, giving to the law of right and wrong a sanction of supreme and religious authority.

PART II.—PHILOSOPHICAL PRINCIPLES.

CHAPTER V.

EGOISM.

SELF-PRESERVATION is a law of human nature which claims the first place in any survey of the rules by which human conduct is governed. We may see reason to reject the system of philosophy which refers the whole conduct of life to self-interest, as narrow from an intellectual point of view, and ignoble from a moral point of view. Nevertheless, there are portions of the conduct of life which must be referred to self-interest, or Egoism; and it is desirable to consider the true functions of Egoism before proceeding to the more important question of its limits as a guide.

In the order of nature, children have an instinct of self-preservation, long before they attain to a consciousness of what they are doing. To shrink from that which causes pain, and seek that which causes pleasure, is in the first instance a spontaneous act. The involuntary closing of the eyelid and contraction of the muscles of the hand are rudiments of that principle which, in its full and conscious development, is termed Egoism.

Education teaches prudence, the skill to measure present loss against future gain in the scale of pleasure; and prudence, according to the Epicurean school of philosophy, is a sufficient principle to regulate the whole conduct of life. By the exercise of prudence, which is a just foresight of consequences, we learn to measure pleasures and pains which are far off, in their true proportions against those which are near. Thus acts of self-denial, of which a child is incapable, become easy to a prudent man. Egoism, guided by prudence, looks

beyond the pleasure of the moment to a more enduring
and substantial pleasure, of which the common name is
Happiness.

It is necessary to understand by Happiness simply a
pleasant state of existence, irrespective of the kind of
pleasure. To introduce any limitation of quality into
the idea of Happiness is to confuse the whole question by an ambiguous use of words. That some pleasures are of a higher order than others, as that the
pleasure of a good conscience is nobler than that of a
good dinner, is a proposition which does not affect the
question of Happiness: nor is Happiness composed of
any fixed elements which can be defined absolutely for
all mankind. The saying of Protagoras—"Man is the
measure of all things," uttered too largely concerning
things in general, might be affirmed truly concerning
Happiness. Man is the measure for himself of that
which makes him happy. To think oneself happy is for
the time to be happy. A child is said to be happy
whenever he is pleased. But it is convenient to distinguish between pleasure and happiness, by applying the
term pleasure to mere incidental emotion, and happiness
to a state more or less prolonged in which pleasure
predominates.

This use of the term Happiness corresponds nearly
with what is found in most philosophical works, although
the whole question is apt to be perplexed by the
assumption that one man's standard of Happiness must
hold good for others; as if Happiness, like sunshine,
were common to all, and only required definition.

Pope, in his "Essay on Man," shows clearly the error
of any such assumption :—

> Oh Happiness ! our being's end and aim !
> Good, pleasure, ease, content ! whate'er thy name !
> That something still which prompts the eternal sigh,
> For which we bear to live, or dare to die ;
> Which still so near us, yet beyond us lies,
> O'erlooked, seen double, by the fool and wise :
> Plant of celestial seed ! if dropped below,
> Say, in what mortal soil thou deign'st to grow ?

*   *   *   *

> Ask of the learn'd the way ? The learn'd are blind :
> This bids to serve, and that to shun, mankind :
> Some place the bliss in action, some in ease,
> Those call it pleasure, and contentment these.

The argument of this celebrated poem is a modified and plausible exposition of the philosophy of Egoism or Self-Interest. Pope lays down as the basis of his ethical theory—

> Two principles in Human Nature reign,
> Self-love to urge, and reason to restrain.

He defines the passions to be modes of self-love, inasmuch as they are all moved by some real or seeming good. He compares the passions to gales by which a ship is impelled, and reason to the chart by which she is navigated.

> Love, hope, and joy, fair pleasure's smiling train,
> Hate, fear, and grief, the family of pain,
> These mixed with art, and to due bounds confined,
> Make and maintain the balance of the mind.

At the same time he contends that, as man is part of a vast system, the welfare of each is inseparable from that of all, so that finally—"True self-love and social are the same," and " Virtue only makes our bliss below."

No one has stated the main propositions of the theory of Egoism with greater epigrammatic force, though others have developed the theory more fully and philosophically.

The strength of the Egoist principle lies in its simplicity. Its weakness is that simplicity is attained by ignoring some vital parts of our moral constitution. There is an apparent completeness and roundness in a theory which professes to bring under a single law the manifold phenomena of human action. Moreover, self-interest is a familiar principle, the operation of which every man may easily recognise. No metaphysical study, no sentimental enthusiasm, is required to teach us to take care for ourselves. For those who dislike sentiment and abstract reasoning it is agreeable to discover how far our intelligent self-interest will take us along the same path which is prescribed by considerations of Duty and Virtue; how an enlarged conception of our own happiness leads us to prefer intellectual pleasures to animal pleasures, and to appreciate highly "the luxury of doing good." Thus, on a superficial view, the principle of Egoism seems to occupy the whole field of human conduct, and to dismiss the idea of moral obligation as a figment. Sure of being able to explain the universe on his own principles, the Epicurean philosopher exclaims triumphantly, " So we tread down religion under foot."*

Yet the principle of Egoism is opposed not only to religious doctrine, but to the common moral sense of mankind. Self-love is never imputed to a man as a praiseworthy quality, but the reverse. Virtue is universally deemed to be the more perfect for being disinterested; and prudence, far from being the highest virtue in popular estimation, is apt to be held cheap when it is indulged at the expense of courage or sympathy. Only philosophers of Falstaff's temper would dare to say, "The better part of valour is discretion." Self-interest is rarely affirmed by any one to be his own principle of conduct; and then only by those who defy the opinion of their neighbours. For the most part men of the world try to dissemble the fact that Egoism is their ruling motive. On no point is there more hypocrisy than on this, from the common desire to be thought unselfish. The open avowal of self-interest is almost confined to the few who are content to stand outside the pale of popular morality; philosophers who despise the multitude as ignorant, and voluptuaries who have lost the sense of shame in the habitual indulgence of their passions.

This popular disrepute raises a fair presumption against the whole system of philosophy which is based on Egoism. It is not easy to believe that a principle, which is so repugnant to the moral sense of mankind at

* Lucretius.

large, can be the true principle of moral conduct. The advocates of Egoism are driven to defend their theory by an appeal to considerations quite apart from sentiment; that is, by showing that Egoism, well understood, fulfils the conditions of social happiness. Accordingly the conclusion which Pope endeavours to prove in his essay is, "that true self-love and social are the same."

If it were possible to prove that the same conduct which social love dictates is to be deduced from rational self-love, there would still remain an irreconcilable difference between the two moral dispositions. Self-love is not the same state of mind as love for others, nor anything like it. Of two nurses in attendance on a rich invalid, one may serve for genuine kindness, the other for hope of a legacy. Their conduct may be the same, yet their moral character is widely different.

In most cases, however, the lines of conduct would diverge; and at all events self-love would refrain from acts of heroic self-devotion, which are productive of the greatest social benefit. It is true that social affection is an important element of happiness, but not always. A selfish man will appreciate the value of having friends, but he will throw over his best friends if, as often happens, their advantage cannot be reconciled with his own.

The case is fairly stated by Mr. Lecky :—

If happiness in any of its forms be the supreme object of life, moderation is the most emphatic counsel of our being, but moderation is as opposed to heroism as to vice. There is no form of intellectual or moral excellence which has not a general tendency to produce happiness if cultivated in moderation. There are very few which, if cultivated to great perfection, have not a tendency directly the reverse.*

Mr. Leslie Stephen expresses a similar opinion :—

"Be good if you would be happy," seems to be the verdict even of worldly prudence ; but it adds in an emphatic aside, "Be not too good."†

Heroic acts of virtue are in most cases attended by suffering on the part of the agent, which is not

---

* "History of Morals," i., 61.   † "Science of Ethics," p. 418.

fully compensated by the consciousness of well-doing.
Although there is for some minds an exquisite pleasure
in this consciousness, and intolerable pain in the consciousness in having acted basely, the mass of mankind
are far from being sensitive to these finer tones of
conscience; and it is not an uncommon event for one
who has made a heroic effort of self-denial in early life
to regret the sacrifice in later years. When the generous
impulse has spent its force, self-love, on reflection, pro-
tests against it: so much opposed are self-interest and
social interest, both in their nature as motives and in
their practical effects as rules of conduct.

Far from accomplishing the general happiness, Egoism
fails to accomplish our own. To be happy, we must not
aim at being happy. Like a shy animal, Happiness
comes to those who are looking another way, and flies
from those who keep their eyes directed towards it.
Nothing is more melancholy than a life devoted to the
pursuit of happiness : and this law of nature holds good,
not only as to vulgar self-indulgence, but even as to
those pleasures which result from virtuous conduct. In
the words of Mr. Lecky :—

A feeling of satisfaction follows the accomplishment of duty for itself ;
but if the duty be performed solely through the expectation of a mental
pleasure, conscience refuses to ratify the bargain.*

In a modern treatise on Ethics, the proposition that
"to be happy you must not aim at happiness" is laid
down as a recognised truth, and termed "The Egoistic
Paradox."†

From a philosophical point of view, the principle of
Egoism has another serious deficiency. Not only does
it fail to supply a satisfactory basis of moral conduct,
but it is very inadequate to describe the appetites,
desires, and affections which compose the animal part of
human nature. Self-love is as distinct from hunger and
thirst as it is distinct from benevolence or gratitude.
On this point Bishop Butler has made some thoughtful
observations :—

---

* "Hist. Morals," i., 38.   † Sidgwick, "Methods of Ethics," p. 133.

Everybody makes a distinction between self-love and the several particular passions, appetites, and affections ; and yet they are often confounded again. That they are totally different will be seen by anyone who will distinguish between the passions and appetites *themselves*, and *endeavouring* after the means of their gratification. Consider the appetite of hunger and the desire of esteem : these being the occasion both of pleasure and pain, the coolest self-love, as well as the appetites and passions themselves, may put us upon the making use of the *proper methods* of obtaining that pleasure and avoiding that pain ; but the *feelings themselves*, the pain of hunger and shame, and the delight from esteem, are no more self-love than they are anything in the world. Though a man hated himself, he would as much feel the pain of hunger as he would that of the gout ; and it is quite supposable there may be creatures with self-love in them to the highest degree, who may be quite insensible and indifferent (as men in some cases are) to the contempt and esteem of those upon whom their happiness does not in some further respects depend.*

Egoism, in short, is founded on a very incomplete survey of the moral constitution of man, and could not be accepted as a philosophical explanation of the problems of life and conduct, even if it were in harmony with the conscience of mankind, which it is not.

Several of the objections which are raised against the sufficiency of Egoism in general as a rule of life, apply to the particular form of Egoism which builds on the hope of happiness in a future state. When Paley gives as a definition of Virtue—" Virtue is the doing good to mankind in obedience to the Will of God, and for the sake of everlasting happiness "—the sentence is marred by its final clause. To act for the sake of everlasting happiness is certainly not a necessary condition of Virtue. In estimating the virtue of philanthropists, such as Howard or Wilberforce, we do not think the less of them if we think them actuated by compassion for others rather than by desire of everlasting happiness for themselves. The desire of happiness is not to be blamed ; for men are so constituted that they must needs wish to be happy ; and it is laudable to aspire to happiness in its noblest and most enduring form. Hence Hope is reckoned among Christian virtues, but it is placed below Charity. There are minds, and those among the best, into which the desire of happiness enters but little, because the consciousness of self is suspended under strong affectionate emotion.

---

* Sermon I. on " Human Nature," Note C. See also Sermon XI.

Desire of Happiness, which on the Egoist theory is
the supreme motive of human action, is neither the only
motive nor the highest. Yet it would be an error, on
the other hand, to lay down rules of conduct without
recognition of the desire of happiness as an integral
part of our nature. There is no sect or school of men
who are really indifferent to their own happiness.
Where they differ is, as to the form in which they
conceive happiness, and the degree in which they
subordinate selfish to unselfish considerations. Egoism
is virtuous or vicious, according as it keeps within or
exceeds its proper functions, which may be summed up
briefly under the two heads of self-preservation and
self-culture. If these are not usually specified as duties,
it is because they are assumed as preliminary conditions
for the fulfilment of duty.

The care of life and health, and the exercise of mental
faculties in arts and sciences, belong to the first steps
in education, before the study of moral philosophy
begins. By such training Egoism is raised above the
vulgar desire of pleasure to the attainment of a high
ideal. A large part of the inventions which have
augmented human happiness have been produced for
the mere delight of the inventor in his own work.
The greatest masterpieces of painting and music, and
the most wonderful discoveries of science, are the spontaneous products of a genius which rarely has any need
of ulterior motives. A Raphael, a Mozart, or a Newton
is pleasing himself while benefiting mankind, not
because he seeks to benefit others, but because his own
happiness takes a form which is beneficial. Egoism in
such cases loses its ignoble quality. It has a certain
sublimity in those who, like Goethe, " rise on stepping
stones of their dead selves to higher things," and it
attains its highest grandeur when a man sets before
himself an ideal standard of human perfection, and
devotes the energies of his whole life to its imitation.

Thus, while rejecting Egoism as a defective principle
of conduct, we must not fail to recognise in it certain

elements of moral goodness which are indispensable.
The need of this caution will appear when we consider
the opposite theory of Altruism.

CHAPTER VI.

ALTRUISM.

SHAKSPERE represents the fiercest of his heroines as
saying :—

> I have given suck, and know
> How tender 'tis to love the babe that milks me.

The affection of parents for their children is the most
familiar example of an unselfish element in human
nature, which cannot properly be regarded as, in any
sense, a mood of self-love. Kindly affection is common
to man with animals. It is one of the chief sources of
happiness, but it is totally distinct from the desire to be
happy, and it is so engrossing as often to be acutely
painful. The sentiments of loyalty and patriotism produce affections of the same class, having for their object
the happiness of others rather than our own. A habit
of life which is under the influence of such affections is
unselfish, and is conveniently described by the term
Altruism, a word which has lately obtained currency as
denoting a moral principle in opposition to Egoism, the
principle of living not for self but for others.

The word Altruism has been brought into use by the
writings of the French philosopher, Auguste Comte, who
takes unselfish affection for the basis of a new "religion
of humanity." "The golden rule of morality, in M.
Comte's religion, is to live for others, ' *Vivre pour autrui.*'
To do as we would be done by, and to love our neighbour
as ourself, are not sufficient for him ; they partake, he
thinks, of the nature of personal calculations. We
should endeavour not to love ourselves at all. We shall
not succeed in it, but we should make the nearest

approach to it possible."* . . . " All education and all moral discipline should have but one object, to make altruism (a word of his own coining) predominate over egoism."*

The subject of the present chapter is to consider how far the principle of Altruism is adequate as a rule of moral conduct, by which the conscience of each man may be adjusted, as a ship's compass is adjusted by astronomical observations. There are two main tests of any moral principle: its accordance with the moral sense of mankind as a motive, and its reasonableness or consistency with human nature as a practical rule.

It has been shown already in reference to the principle of Egoism that the voice of society pronounces strongly in favour of love for others in preference to self-love, as a laudable motive of action. The words unselfish and selfish convey at once to our ears the praise and blame which is attached to them respectively by the moral sense of mankind. If the alternative lay simply between Altruism and Egoism the choice could not be doubtful, so far as it depends on comparison of motives. All that can be urged by reason on the side of self-preservation, self-culture, and the pursuit of happiness, would be overborne by the strong appeal which is made to the affections and the conscience, which is made in the name of love, when its various forms, parental, filial, conjugal, fraternal, are combined in one principle of living for others.

But the principle of Altruism is weakened by disunion. Its several elements are not combined together. Filial and conjugal affection, for instance, are frequently so balanced that Egoism can turn the scale either way without incurring the reproach of selfishness.

> My noble father,
> I do perceive here a divided duty :
> To you I am bound for life and education :
> My life and education both do learn me
> How to respect you : you are the lord of duty,
> I am hitherto your daughter : but here's my husband.

---

* Mill's Essays on Auguste Comte and Positivism, p. 138.

Private and public obligations are apt to come in conflict. The proverbial saying that "fathers of families are capable of anything," implies that family affection makes men traitors to their country. A similar reproach is conveyed by the stigma which is attached in popular opinion to the word "nepotism." A more familiar proverb, "Charity begins at home," expresses a common sentiment that those who are nearest to us in blood have the first claim to our kindly affections. So, if we appeal to the common sense of mankind in favour of Altruism, we shall find its approval given under narrow limitations. The same persons who praise self-denial as a virtue, are often found blaming as a vice the liberal charity, which passes over those who are nearest in blood. According to the popular standard of morality, a man ought to deny himself for the sake of others, but he ought not to deny his children for the sake of the children of others. We praise him if he gives his own dinner to the poor ; but we blame him if he gives his children's dinner to the poor. Whenever our natural affections come into conflict with loyalty or patriotism, or comprehensive philanthropy, the rule of living for others becomes perplexed. What would have been deemed a sin under ordinary circumstances, appears in the light of a duty, according as one or the other affection gains ascendency. Thus the Jacobite ballads breathe a spirit of devotion to the house of Stuart, which sets at nought the most tender ties of nature :—

> I ance had sons, I now hae nane ;
> I bred them, toiling sairly ;
> And I wad bear them a' again,
> And lose them a', for Charlie !

Altruism is therefore too vague a principle to be applied to conduct as a practical rule, or even as a motive, unless the numerous and often conflicting claims of society can be adjusted in their true proportion. The tendency of civilisation is always to widen the circle of duty, giving a more important place to public duties in

3

comparison with those of kindred and private friendship.
An illiterate peasant, called to give evidence in a court
of justice, will often think less of his obligations as a
witness than of the fact that the prisoner at the bar is a
neighbour in trouble. His conscience is fully alive to
the fact that he has to perform an important duty, but
he understands his duty in a different sense from that
which justice dictates. He holds himself bound to
screen his friend, and in giving false evidence for that
purpose takes no shame to himself. Abstract truth,
abstract justice, public welfare, public safety, are conceptions beyond the range of his mind, and so he follows
the light of his own conscience, while he seems utterly
without moral sense if tried by a different standard.

In the romance of "John Inglesant," the interest of
the story turns on the unselfish fraud of the hero, who
falsely declares himself to have forged the royal signa-
ture to a commission which the king wishes to disavow.
The effect of his Jesuit training shows itself in an
Altruism, which is ready to sacrifice both life and honour
with unreserved self-devotion to the person of his sove-
reign, regardless of his country's welfare.

Of all modes of human conduct, that which is regulated
by the dictates of a secret society is perhaps the most
unselfish, and also the most immoral. Less extreme in
both respects, but not much less, is the spirit of personal
fidelity to a prince or the chief of a clan. By the nature
of the case it is impossible to deduce any general principle of duty from the subjection of self to others, when
duty is represented by the variable will of a superior.

A more definite form is given to the abstract principle
of Altruism by two great ideas, the idea of a National
Society, or Commonwealth, and the idea of an Universal
Society. The former is the basis of the morality expounded in Cicero's treatise "De Officiis;" the latter is the
basis of the speculations of M. Comte, in his "Politique
Positive."

According to Cicero, patriotism is the supreme motive
of human action, and all private affections are subordinate to the claims of our country.

Cari sunt parentes, cari liberi, propinqui, familiares ; sed omnes omnium caritates patria una complexa est ; pro quâ quis bonus dubitet mortem oppetere, si ei sit profuturus ?*

Cicero wrote as a citizen of a republic which extended to the limits of the civilised world. He wrote also with a reverential affection for the men of a former age who had made Rome so great, and with a burning indignation at the factiousness and selfishness of his contemporaries. Soon after his time patriotism died out from Roman history. Tacitus was one of the last to give a muffled utterance to the sentiments which had animated the heroes of old Rome. For more than a thousand years the patriotic spirit appeared to be almost extinct; and though it has revived in modern Europe, it has been confined within comparatively narrow limits. The subdivision of the continent into a number of rival states has made it impossible for any philosophical writer to accept the maxims which satisfied Cicero. Popular enthusiasm can be aroused by the idea of nationality, as we have seen in Switzerland, Poland, Ireland, Greece, Italy, and Germany; but as the basis of moral philosophy a wider principle is required. No idea less comprehensive than that of an universal society can be entertained by anyone whose view extends beyond the borders of his own land.

How this idea of Universal Humanity is developed by Comte is explained concisely as follows by John Stuart Mill,† in a friendly review of his philosophy :—

The power which may be acquired over the mind by the idea of the general interest of the human race, both as a source of emotion and as a motive to conduct, many have perceived ; but we know not if anyone, before M. Comte, realised so fully as he has done all the majesty of which that idea is susceptible. It ascends into the unknown past, embraces the manifold present, and descends into the indefinite unforesecable future. Forming a collective Existence, without assignable beginning or end, it appeals to that feeling of the Infinite which is deeply rooted in human nature, and which seems necessary to the imposingness of all our highest conceptions. Of the vast unrolling web of human life, the part best known to us is irrevocably past. This we can no longer serve, but we can still love : it comprises for most of us the far greater number of those who have loved us, or from whom we have received benefits, as well as the long series

---

* "De Officiis," i., 17.   † "Auguste Comte and Positivism," p. 135.

of those who, by their labours and sacrifices for mankind, have deserved to
be held in everlasting and grateful remembrance. As M. Comte truly says,
the highest minds, even now, live in thought with the great dead far more
than with the living ; and, next to the dead, with those ideal human beings
yet to come, whom they are never destined to see. If we honour as we
ought those who have served mankind in the past, we shall feel that we are
also working for those benefactors by serving that to which their lives were
devoted. And when reflection, guided by history, has taught us the
intimacy of the connexion of every age of humanity with every other,
making us to see in the earthly destiny of mankind the playing out of a
great drama, or the action of a prolonged epic, all the generations of mankind become indissolubly united into a single image, combining all the
power over the mind of the idea of Posterity, with our best feelings towards
the living world which surrounds us, and towards the predecessors who
have made us what we are. That the ennobling power of this great conception may have its full efficacy, we should, with M. Comte, regard the
Grand Être, Humanity, or Mankind, as composed, in the past, solely of
those who, in every age and variety of position, have played their part
worthily in life.

No better or more favourable statement of the
principle of Altruism, in its most highly developed
philosophical form, could be given. The sublimity of
the idea of Universal Humanity, and its power as an
incentive to virtuous action, can be sufficiently understood from this passage, and are indisputable. We
have to consider, however, not only the grandeur of
this idea, but its sufficiency to stand alone, as an
independent principle of morality. From this point of
view it requires critical examination.

Two important questions occur : How far does the
doctrine of Universal Humanity commend itself to the
conscience of mankind as an inspiring motive? and
how far does it supply a reasonable and consistent rule
of conduct? Neither of these questions admits of a
satisfactory answer.

The conception of mankind as one vast Being is
hardly to be entertained at all without a more than
ordinary mental effort. It is extremely difficult to
imagine past and future 'generations, together with the
present, as constituents of this ideal Being. A conception such as this needs to be associated with some other
doctrine, less remote from the experience of common
life, to touch the hearts of men. So, when a similar
principle, that of Universal Fraternity, fascinated the

French nation in the era of the Revolution, it was associated with Liberty and Equality; that is, with the abolition of feudal tyranny, with the removal of social distinctions which were a daily insult, and of monopolies which drove men through starvation to the verge of madness. Fraternity was then hailed as part of a dream of a renovated state of society, in which king, aristocracy, and clergy should be swept away. In a more sober state of society, when the wages of labour are secure to the labourer, and degrees of rank have ceased to press heavily on the poor, the idea of Universal Fraternity inspires comparatively faint enthusiasm. There is little to choose in this respect between the Fraternity of Rousseau and the Altruism of Comte, except that the latter is more systematic, an advantage which may commend it to speculative philosophers, but is far over the heads of the multitude.

Again, the reasonableness and consistency of M. Comte's doctrine suffer by his arbitrary choice of certain names as representative of Humanity in the past. The selection of "those who have played their part worthily in life," assumes a power of deciding what is worthy or unworthy, which begs the whole question as to what is the governing principle of morals. The entire scheme depends on the manner in which this choice is exercised, for the ideal of Humanity is defined by means of the representative names which are taken. M. Comte's calendar of names exhibits his own ideal, but not that of any one who differs from him. Mankind are far from being agreed as to the chief characteristics of worth. If Dante, Milton, and Goethe, to take three of the most discerning intellects, were to nominate "those who have played their part worthily in life," their choice would differ widely in the result. A system of morals, in which so much depends on individual judgment, has no right to profess universality. It is really eclectic, and its pretended comprehensiveness is an illusion.

There is an obvious resemblance between Comte's Altruism and Christian morality, which makes it important to note the particulars in which they are

agreed, and those in which they are opposed. They
have in common the inculcation of brotherly love as a
supreme duty, the worship and imitation of an ideal
Humanity, the separation of a select body from the
world at large. But Comte's system is in other respects
not only distinct, but antagonistic to Christianity. God
and Christ are excluded with a jealous intolerance.
What is retained is a Brotherhood without a Fatherhood,
a Body without a Head. What Comte offers as an ideal
of Humanity is a Torso of Christianity, which he has
mutilated. It is a curious contradiction of the first
principle of Altruism, that the modern gospel of
unselfishness should be a selfish plagiarism, in which a
large part of the Christian morality is republished with
the Author's name expunged.

On one point, however, Comte's Altruism advances
beyond the limits of Christian doctrine. He teaches
that, instead of loving our neighbour as ourselves, we
should endeavour not to love ourselves at all. And this,
which is the most original feature in Comte's doctrine,
is claimed by his followers as an improvement on
Christianity.

A fair comparison of the two will show that this
fancied superiority is a dream of the study, and betrays
a want of acquaintance with human nature. To exclude
self-love is to take away the natural provision for self-
preservation and self-culture, which are necessary conditions of the welfare of society. On the other hand,
to make self-love a standard of brotherly love, as in the
precept, "Thou shalt love thy neighbour as thyself," is
to supply the most effective means by which brotherly
love can promote its own object. Altruism without
Egoism would be a vague yearning for the happiness of
others, without any clear idea of happiness, what it is,
or how it is to be obtained. If we suppose a company
of pedestrians, each troubled in mind to be sure that his
companions' boots fit them comfortably, and indifferent
to his own, we should have a picture of a state of society
in which Egoism was extinguished and Altruism
remained. It would be necessary to find some kind

of substitute for Egoism, in order to keep alive the
sensibility to pleasure and pain, which is as necessary
for the happiness of others as for our own. A man who
wishes to make others happy has more power to do so
in proportion as he feels sympathy in their pleasure;
and thus Egoism has a function preparatory to Altruism.
On strictly Altruist principles arts and sciences would
languish. That which impelled Columbus to the discovery of America, and led on the inventors of the printing
press and the steam engine, was not a prevision of the
social benefits to follow, but rather an unsatisfied desire
of the mind to accomplish a noble object.

The rarity of unselfishness, and the great value of
Altruism for the good of the world, lead us to praise
actions which are prompted by generous emotion, without
pausing to inquire whether they conform to sound general
rules of conduct. A remarkable instance took place
lately, in the shipwreck of the *Cyprian*, on the Welsh
coast. The captain saw the vessel breaking up rapidly,
and had provided himself with a life-belt in expectation
of being cast into the sea, when he saw a poor boy beside
him, who was not one of the crew, but had obtained a
passage in the ship as a stowaway. He flung the life-belt
to the boy, and presently both were in the water. The
captain was drowned: the boy came safe to shore. Who
does not applaud the generosity of the act? So long as
selfishness is common among men, and unselfishness
has the rarity of a precious metal, we must praise even
the extravagance of self-devotion. Yet, if conduct is to
be governed by general rules, it would hardly be laid
down that a captain, who had done his duty to his ship,
should in all cases prefer the safety of others to his own;
and it might even be necessary in the interests of society
to censure the imitation of Captain Strachan's example,
if it were common, as the Montanists were censured for
courting martyrdom.

The consideration of Altruism as a principle of conduct
leads to no result more definite than is suggested by this
story. As a motive of action, it is indispensable to the
highest virtue, and it is invested with a moral beauty

and dignity with which no form of Egoism can compare. As a practical rule it leaves much to be defined with reference to the rival claims of family, of neighbourhood, and of the public. Moreover, the definition of Altruist principles, in proportion as it is logically complete, tends to lose the hold on popular sympathy which distinguishes the same principles in a simpler form. Altruism, in the form of parental or filial affection, of pity for the poor and weak and friendless, touches a responsive chord in every human heart. Altruism, in the form of loyalty and patriotism, is the source of many heroic actions which all the world admires. But as the circle widens the force weakens, and the love of Universal Humanity is only effective when it draws its spiritual energy from some other source than abstract philosophy.

CHAPTER VII.

UTILITARIANISM.

" THE greatest happiness of the greatest number," is Bentham's well-known formula for solving the problems of moral conduct. Bentham acknowledged himself to be indebted for this phrase to Dr. Priestley, who published his " Essay on Government" in 1768. " He there introduced, in italics, as the only reasonable and proper object of government, *the greatest happiness of the greatest number.* By this expression of Priestley, Bentham conceived that his own principles on the subject of morality, public and private, were determined." *

In Bentham's writings this principle is termed the "principle of utility;" and the system of moral philosophy of which it is the foundation is now commonly known by the name of Utilitarianism.

---

* Whewell, "Lectures on the History of Moral Philosophy in England," p. 190.

To set aside motives for results, to study Happiness instead of Virtue or Duty, was not reserved for modern thinkers. Lucretius claimed for his master Epicurus the glory of bringing light out of darkness, by teaching men to be happy; and probably unrecorded sages before Epicurus had given utterance to many true sayings on the same subject. All animated nature expresses, articulately or inarticulately, its sympathy with the Epicurean doctrine. The value of Bentham's formula consists in its application to a complex state of society, as a means of simplifying moral questions. Utilitarianism arbitrates between Egoism and Altruism, and serves to define the variable dictates of moral intuition as to justice and other cardinal virtues. How far the "Greatest Happiness Principle" is a true and sufficient guide of moral conduct is to be considered in this chapter. I propose to examine its advantages and deficiencies, not in the crude and exaggerated form in which it is stated by Bentham himself, but in the exposition of his more judicious disciple J. S. Mill.

The Creed which accepts as the foundation of Morals, Utility, or the Greatest Happiness Principle, holds that actions are right in proportion as they tend to promote happiness, wrong as they tend to produce the reverse of happiness. By happiness is intended pleasure, and the absence of pain ; by unhappiness, pain, and the privation of pleasure.*

According to the Greatest Happiness Principle, the ultimate end, with reference to and for the sake of which all other things are desirable (whether we are considering our own good or that of other people), is an existence exempt as far as possible from pain, and as rich as possible in enjoyments, both in quantity and quality ; the test of quality, and the rule for measuring it against quantity, being the preference felt by those who, in their opportunities of experience, to which must be added their habits of self-consciousness and observation, are best furnished with the means of comparison This being, according to the utilitarian opinion, the end of human action, is necessarily also the standard of morality ; which may accordingly be defined the rules and precepts for human conduct, by the observance of which an existence such as has been described might be, to the greatest extent possible, secured to all mankind ; and not to them only, but, so far as the nature of things admits, to the whole sentient creation.†

Comparing this principle with simple Egoism, or simple Altruism, the most obvious characteristic is that it deals

---

* Mill, " Utilitarianism," p. 9.   † Ibid., p. 17.

with actions rather than agents, and in so doing offers a
practical compromise between Egoism, which subordinates the happiness of others to our own, and Altruism,
which excludes all regard to our own happiness. On
the principle of "the greatest happiness of the greatest
number," questions concerning selfish or unselfish conduct are to be decided by a numerical test, "everybody
to count for one, nobody for more than one."*

Another practical advantage which is claimed for the
Utilitarian principle is, that it gives a criterion in some
questions concerning justice as to which simple moral
intuition is at fault. The question, What is justice?
has been one of the chief problems of moral philosophy
from Plato's "Republic" to the present day. Our common
ideas of justice are shaped by the influences of custom
and positive law, which vary with every country and
with every generation of men. Where the custom of
primogeniture prevails, equal division is unjust in the
eyes of those who look to custom as the rule of justice;
and, on the other hand, rights of primogeniture seem
unjust to those who are accustomed to a law of equal
division. Slavery, the franchise, the criminal code, are
matters with which the law deals by positive enactment,
and whatever the law has enacted is taken for justice
by the multitude, whose standard of justice is merely
conventional. That this standard is not absolute and
final is plain from the consideration that it alters with
every alteration in the law. Every legislative act is a
recognition of an ideal of justice more perfect than the
law as it stands. If a bill is introduced emancipating
slaves, or extending the franchise, or altering the criminal
law, the promoters of every such amendment appeal to
principles of justice which the existing state of the law
fails to satisfy, and the passing of the act ratifies appeals
of this kind.

Thrasymachus, in Plato's "Republic," defines justice
as "the interest of the stronger," a definition which,
however superficial, has an element of historical truth,

---

* Bentham, quoted by Mill, p. 91.

inasmuch as the strongest make the laws upon which the popular idea of justice is modelled. But the claims of the weak in opposition to the strong are maintained by the Utilitarian philosophy. To define justice as what is expedient for the greatest number, is the Utilitarian answer to the question, What is justice?

The effect of this principle on legislation and morals is manifest. It is no accidental coincidence which has associated Utilitarianism with humanity in the treatment of prisoners, with extension of civil rights, with the advocacy of peace and arbitration in international disputes. Where abstract justice, as interpreted by intuition, approves of ancient custom, Utilitarian morality breaks through custom, in the interest of the many against the few, of the oppressed against the oppressor. Where an intuitive sense of justice breathes mere vengeance, Utilitarian morality interposes with a prudent consideration of the horrors of war. Comparing the present state of society with that of a century ago, we observe that the moral intuitions of the English people have been transformed, under the influence of the Greatest Happiness Principle. Domestic slavery, which seemed to Aristotle part of the order of nature, and was a recognised institution till lately in America, has been abolished by the force of an altered public opinion. Women and children, and even animals, have come under the special protection of the law, through an enlarged conception of justice, to which Utilitarian philosophy has contributed.

In these respects Utilitarianism appears to advantage. As to another important department of morals, namely, truth or veracity, the use of the Utilitarian formula is doubtful. At first sight, indeed, an estimate of "the greatest happiness of the greatest number" may appear to be a short and easy method of answering the crucial questions of veracity which have perplexed moralists; such, for instance, as whether promises extorted by violence are binding? Whether a seller is bound to disclose to the buyer all that he knows concerning the value of his commodity? Whether extreme cases, like

that of the escape of an innocent man, justify a lie?
Questions of this kind can be discussed on Utilitarian
principles more conveniently than on principles of
intuitive morality. But they cannot be decided wisely
without laying emphasis on the value of general rules
and of moral habits, far beyond anything which can be
deduced from Utilitarianism. Much may be said, even
on Utilitarian principles, as to the importance of good
faith and honesty to social happiness, as to the misery
which falsehood brings on those who practise it and
their neighbours. So far, indeed, Utilitarianism is
favourable to veracity. Yet the calculation of results,
which is an essential part of the system, is opposed
to the formation of a moral habit of truthfulness
without regard to consequences. Veracity on Utilitarian
principles would be limited to cases in which truth-
telling was demonstrably expedient. To lay down as a
moral axiom, "Veracity is always expedient," would be
contrary to the Utilitarian principle, which admits of no
universal axioms, but leaves every rule of conduct to be
drawn from results. Besides, the habit of truthfulness
on Utilitarian principles falls short of the highest order
of virtue. Archbishop Whately has stated the case
concisely in saying, "Honesty is the best policy; but a
man who acts honestly for this reason is not an honest
man."

When we turn from actions to agents, and consider
Utilitarianism as a rule of virtue, we find it wanting in
some vital elements. It could hardly be stated more
ingeniously than in a group of aphorisms by Bentham :—

The best way to be comfortable is to make others comfortable.
The best way to make them comfortable is to appear to love them.
The best way to appear to love them is to love them in reality.

However true in fact these propositions may be, the
calculated love which they inspire cannot be very warm
or genuine.

There is a difference between goodness of conduct
and goodness of character of which Utilitarianism
fails to take account. As a moral principle it lies

pen to the criticism that, "if the excellence of virtue consists solely in its utility, or tendency to promote the happiness of men, a machine, a fertile field, or a navigable river would all possess in a very high degree the elements of virtue."* And if it be replied that virtue consists in the intelligent wish to promote happiness, this reply is open to the objection that actions and not wishes are the proper subject of Utilitarianism, which seems in its rigid sense to leave no room for virtue in character apart from useful conduct. Virtue may be defined on Utilitarian principles as a habit of conduct which is for the greatest happiness of the greatest number. In ordinary cases particular results are of small consequence in comparison with the maintenance of general rules, and therefore the rule of utility will agree with the rule of conscience. But there are cases in which the results of a single act are so momentous as to be fairly balanced against the advantage of keeping a general rule unbroken, and in these extreme cases the rule of conscience and the rule of utility are opposed.

A man of high eminence, the hope of a great nation, is assassinated by a disappointed place-hunter. The whole civilised world denounces the act as an abominable crime, and deplores it as a public calamity. By and by, however, the victim's patience and many noble qualities, evinced during a prolonged time of suffering, elicit a sympathy which leads to unforeseen consequences. To his own people he appears as the martyr of a cause, which gains more popularity by his death than it could have gained by his life. From other nations also comes a kindly sympathy, which has drawn together the two branches of the Anglo-American race as they never were drawn together before. Are we therefore to reverse our judgment of the murder? On principles of utility we might hesitate. But our conscience refuses to accept a principle which makes no distinction between the virtues of the murdered man and the crime which served to make those virtues known more widely.

---

* Lecky, "History of Morals," i., 41.

Both parts of Bentham's formula are open to serious
objection. The term Happiness is not well chosen to
denote the highest and noblest objects of human action.
It is a word of which the homely sense is the most
obvious. Although it may be understood by Utilitarians
of generous mind to comprehend all that can be desired
in an ideal state of existence, its familiar use tends to
associate the word Happiness with such pleasures as
mankind at large are accustomed to enjoy; according to
Pope's description :—

> Know, all the good that individuals find,
> Or God and nature meant to mere mankind :
> Reason's whole pleasure, all the joys of sense,
> Lie in three words, health, peace, and competence.

Hence the "Greatest Happiness Principle" is deficient in
the qualities which kindle enthusiasm, and animate men
to live well in opposition to their natural inclination. It
is essentially prosaic, not to say gross; and this prosaic
character is impressed more strongly by the frequent
use of the term utility, which suggests to the ear
common-place usefulness, however largely the word may
be amplified by high-minded Utilitarians.

There is likewise a legitimate objection to be raised
against the numerical test, which is a special characteristic of the Utilitarian principle, "everybody to count
for one, nobody for more than one." The reason and
conscience of mankind are far from assenting to this
uniform level of equality. Most men share the opinion
of that ancient Greek lecturer, who was consoled for the
desertion of all his hearers but one, when he observed
that the remaining one was Plato. A fine tragedy of
Calderon's, "The Constant Prince," deals with this very
question, the value of a noble life in comparison with
ordinary lives. The play turns on the offer of an
important city as ransom for a captive, who refuses to
accept liberty on these terms. It concludes, in the
loftiest spirit of Spanish chivalry, with the acceptance
of his dead body as an equivalent for the best of the
living prisoners on the other side. Nor is it only in

romantic fiction that the rule of equality is felt to be inapplicable. During the siege of Haarlem, in 1573, the daily allowance to the population was a pound of bread to each man, and half a pound to each woman; and when William of Orange projected a desperate expedition for the relief of the city, he was opposed by the general remonstrances of the other cities and of the soldiers whom he was to lead. "They would not consent that a life so precious, so indispensable to the existence of Holland, should be needlessly hazarded. It was important to succour Haarlem; but the Prince was of more value than many lives."*

Whatever may be the true solution of this difficult problem, it is certain that an Alexander or a Napoleon cannot be regarded as a single unit in computing the pleasures and pains of mankind. The influence which great men have on the aggregate happiness of the world makes necessary some modification of the "greatest number" principle. If the presence of one man with an army in the field is equivalent to a reinforcement of ten thousand men, it is idle to affect to treat him as a single individual. For good or for evil men are constituted unequal in most respects; in their power to make others happy, and their power to receive happiness from others. Of such inequalities in human nature the principle of Utility takes little or no account.

On the whole, Utilitarianism falls very far short of a complete philosophy of morals. The popular prejudice which dislikes Utilitarian views as ignoble, is not altogether groundless, for, although its language may be construed in an elevated sense, the vulgar sense is nearest at hand. Its chief value is in legislation, where it counteracts the tyrannical ideas of privileged classes. As a principle of morals, in which not only conduct but character is to be regulated, Utilitarianism is deficient. Neither the idea of Virtue nor the idea of Duty is to be deduced from the principle of Utility. We must look to some other source for motives to set in action the

---

* Motley's "Rise of the Dutch Republic," ch. viii.

conduct which Utilitarian philosophy prescribes. Even when that conduct is most agreeable to reason, a stronger appeal to conscience and imagination is required to enforce it.

What is wanting to the Utilitarian system is partially supplied by the theory of Evolution, which will form the subject of the next chapter, considered in its application to morals.

CHAPTER VIII.

EVOLUTION.

By the word Evolution is denoted a tendency in the universe towards a more perfect state. Combining the idea of the universe as a Kosmos, "one harmonious whole," according to Humboldt's definition, with the idea of Growth, as we see it exhibited in the vegetable world from seed to fruit, we can form an approximate conception of the meaning of Evolution, as used in modern philosophy.

Evolution is defined by Dr. Johnson as

"1. The act of unrolling or unfolding.

2. The series of things unrolled or unfolded."

He gives an example from Henry More's "Divine Dialogues":—

The whole evolution of ages, from everlasting to everlasting, is so collectedly and presentifically represented to God at once, as if all things that ever were, are, or shall be, were at this very instant really present.

In the more technical use of the word by Mr. Herbert Spencer and his followers, Evolution implies much more than sequence of events, which is apparently all that is intended in this passage.

The points which are of most importance to be observed, in considering the application of the principle of Evolution to morals, are three:—

1. That man is part of an infinite and changing universe.

2. That our character is partly the result of inherited, partly of acquired qualities.

3. That the perfect development of individual man and of society, in mutual harmony, is the highest conceivable good.

These three propositions indicate the chief features of a moral theory which is allied to Utilitarianism, but which has the advantage of a more comprehensive basis, and a larger scope. For our present inquiry it will suffice, without investigating the subject more closely, to consider these three propositions in their bearing on human conduct.

1. The grandeur of the conception of mankind as part of an infinite and changing universe, is in itself impressive, and it gains strength from the analogies which are supplied by the various departments of nature. One of the earliest poetical comparisons is between the growth of human life and that of plants;* and one of the earliest philosophical comparisons is between the life of individual men and societies of men.† There is a general tendency in human thought, especially of late years, towards a conception similar to that which is expressed by Tennyson :—

> I doubt not through the ages one increasing purpose runs,
> And the thoughts of men are widened with the process of the suns.

So far as Evolution gives a name to this idea of progress combined with order pervading the universe, it is in harmony with the deepest convictions of most thoughtful men in the present generation. In this respect Evolution satisfies one condition of a moral principle, in which Utilitarianism fails. It lifts up the mind at once to a higher speculative level, from which the utilities of the passing hour appear in their true relation to the utilities which concern the future. Philosophically this is an advantage : practically it is not without disadvantages. To climb to an Alpine height

---

* Homer, "Iliad," vi., 146. † Plato, "Republic," viii.

4

from which cities appear mere spots on a boundless plain, is a cure for the faults of narrow sympathy, but it fails to inspire warm sympathies on a larger scale. Nationality seems dwarfed to little more than a parochial sentiment in view of the interests of universal humanity, but this does not tend of itself to make men practically humane. And if we proceed further, to contemplate mankind as only one of many species of organized life upon the terrestrial planet, the gain is intellectual rather than moral. Moral law loses some of its dignity in proportion to the diminished scale in which man, with all his hopes and duties, is presented to our imagination. Thus the tendency of large speculative views concerning human life is not altogether favourable to good conduct, inasmuch as they relax our moral energies.

Whatever may be the scientific value of the principle of Evolution, its moral value must be judged by its power to govern the will. Comprehensive philosophy is less effective in this respect than the popular rules of neighbourly duty, which require a man to be a good son, a good brother, a good citizen, and so on. Morality is likely to be dissipated into space by resting on a generalisation too wide for the grasp of the human mind. It is only a few who can rise to the height of the principle of Evolution, and those few are apt to suffer morally from the want of the homely discipline of temper and character which a less ambitious training provides. Philosophers of the rarest intellectual qualities are often less fitted to their social environment than ordinary men. The trials of schoolboy life are in some respects more effective in subduing fretfulness, selfishness, and vanity, than the whole circle of the sciences. While the speculative intellect aspires to rise above the prepossessions of nationality and religion, poor human nature yields to the personal influences of flattery or contradiction, an ill-cooked dinner, or an east wind. Such is the mixture of greatness and littleness in man: " a thinking reed," as Pascal terms him.

Magnanimity of character requires something more than breadth of philosophical views. Nevertheless, the study of morals on the dispassionate principles which belong to the theory of Evolution, surveying morals as part of the natural history of man, ought to counteract some of the prejudices which are most opposed to justice, mercy, and truth.

The following passage from Herbert Spencer's "Study of Sociology" will serve as an illustration of the value of this method. He is speaking of "the one-sidedness shown in the traditions of each nation concerning the barbarity of nations it has fought with":—

As in old times the Normans, vindictive themselves, were shocked at the vindictiveness of the English when driven to bay ; so in recent times the French have enlarged on the atrocities committed by Spanish guerillas, and the Russians on the atrocities the Circassians perpetrated. In this conflict between the views of those who commit savage acts, and the views of those on whom they are committed, we clearly perceive the bias of patriotism where both sides are aliens, but we fail to perceive it where we are ourselves concerned as actors. Every one old enough remembers the reprobation vented here when the French dealt so cruelly with Arabs who refused to submit—lighting fires at the mouths of caves in which they had taken refuge ; but we do not see a like barbarity in deeds of our own in India, such as the executing a group of rebel Sepoys by fusillade, and then setting fire to the heap of them because they were not all dead, or in the wholesale shootings and burnings of houses, after the suppression of the Jamaica insurrection. Listen to what is said about such deeds in our own colonies, and you will find that habitually they are held to have been justified by the necessities of the case. Listen to what is said about such deeds when other nations are guilty of them, and you find the same persons indignantly declare that no alleged necessities could form a justification.*

2. That our character is the result, partly of inherited and partly of acquired qualities, is a familiar truth in general terms.

Fortes creantur fortibus et bonis . . .
Doctrina sed vim promovet insitam.

But the development of this principle, with reference to the dictates of conscience, is a recent and important contribution to moral science. That the acquired knowledge, which is gained by the experience of one generation, is transmitted in the form of a moral intuition to the next, is a theory which goes far to solve one of the chief problems of moral philosophy. Moralists allied to the Stoic school have usually regarded our approval of certain virtues, such as fortitude, temperance, and

---

* Spencer, "Study of Sociology," p. 208.

justice, as innate. The Epicureans and others have held on the contrary that our perception of these virtues is not intuitive, but a result of our experience of the social benefits which follow upon them. In favour of the former opinion, it is urged that the approval of our conscience is more quickly formed, and more absolute, than it could be if its judgments depended upon our private experience. In favour of the latter opinion, it is urged that the dictates of our conscience are too vague and variable and dependent on local custom, to be explained by the theory of Innate Ideas. But the two opposite views are to a great extent reconciled by the principle of a hereditary growth of moral sentiments. The supposition that innate ideas are really inherited ideas explains their spontaneousness, and also their dependence on local custom. On this supposition the experience of parents is transmitted to the children, not only in the processes of education, but partially in the very blood ; so that later generations are born with an aptitude to see intuitively what their forefathers learned through much labour and pains. This theory of development of moral faculties by hereditary descent is in harmony with some of the most curious phenomena of instinct, and has been so well established in the works of Mr. Spencer and others, that it must take place as a substantial addition to the elements of moral philosophy.

3. The perfect development of individual man and of society, in mutual harmony, is the highest conceivable good. This is a principle which belongs to Platonic philosophy, but which assumes a more scientific form in connexion with the theory of Evolution. One important application of this principle is to adjust the opposite claims of Egoism and Altruism. A moralist who aims at perfection, both individual and social, stands upon advantageous ground in discussing all that can be urged on either side. His aim is to discover " those conditions under which only associated activities can be so carried on, that the complete living of each consists with, and conduces to, the complete living of all."* He is thus prepared to vindicate the rights of

---

* Spencer, " Data of Ethics," p. 148.

society against the encroachments of Egoism; and at the same time to assert the necessity of self-preservation against the impulsive extravagence of Altruism.

The care of health is an instance of the legitimate claims of Egoism, which are too often disregarded to the injury of the individual and of society also.

Now the case is that of a labourer, who, conscientiously continuing his work under a broiling sun, spite of violent protest from his feelings, dies of sunstroke, and leaves his family a burden to the parish. Now the case is that of a clerk, whose eyes permanently fail from overstraining, or who, daily writing for hours after his fingers are painfully cramped, is attacked with "scrivener's palsy," and, unable to write at all, sinks with aged parents into poverty which friends are called upon to mitigate. And now the case is that of a man devoted to public ends, who, shattering his health by ceaseless application, fails to achieve all that he might have achieved by a more reasonable apportionment of his time between labour on behalf of others and ministration to his own ends.*

Thus a wise consideration of the welfare of others throws us back on those primary impulses of nature which dictate the preservation of life and health, and the frugal use of our talents of every kind. Egoism is a bad master, but a good servant when disciplined for public service. Moreover, Altruism is guided to refinements of benevolence, not obvious at first si ht, by means of reflection on our own experience of happiness. If we have found any pleasure in the act of giving pleasure to others, a true Altruism will take care that others may share in this pleasure of giving. In such a state of reciprocal giving and receiving, which is not uncommon in a well-nurtured and affectionate family, the conflicting elements of Egoism and Altruism are as nearly as possible reconciled. On this subject Mr. Spencer has well said—"That which the best human nature is capable of, is within the reach of human nature at large."†

The philosophy of Evolution is highly suggestive to minds which are predisposed to seek for truth and goodness. It assimilates what is most valuable in Utilitarianism, with an ideal aim of which Utility gives no sign. One thing, however, is wanting, and that the most vital of all. It wants momentum. The moral

---

* Spencer, "Data of Ethics," p. 195.   † Ibid., p. 257.

sentiments of mankind respond to any appeal better
than to that which is made in the name of Evolution.
This deficiency is frankly admitted in a recent exposition of the evolutionist theory of morals:—

The scientific moralist has fulfilled his task when he has explained what
virtue and vice naturally are, what are their normal consequences to society
and the individual, and what are the conditions under which they are
generated. He has done all that he can do if he has laid down true
propositions upon such matters. . . . . But it is an error to try the
scientific moralist by the test of the political moralist.*

To analyse the phenomena of growth in plants, or in
animals, or in the moral constitution of man, or in the
succession of various social states from the lowest
barbarism to the highest civilisation, is among the most
instructive studies that can engage our attention. Yet
it is a study which omits at least one of the supreme
questions of moral philosophy, "Why must I do what
is right?" The Evolution theory makes no popular
appeal to the conscience, and knows nothing of Duty,
content to exhibit a gradual progress in nature, as in
the specimens of a vast museum. A man must needs
ask himself, "Is this progress, or tendency to progress
in the universe, a law for me?" "If so, why am I
obliged to obey it, whether I will or no? Why may I
not find my greatest private satisfaction in a course
opposed to the general stream?"

To questions like these the principle of Evolution
gives no articulate answer. It presents an ideal picture
of a highly developed society; but if we do not like the
picture, there is nothing more to be said. We are free
to make some other choice, and to govern our life
accordingly. What is true of philosophical systems in
general is true especially of this, that it provides no
strong motive to support the weak against temptation,
or to deter the violent from crime. To make a coward
brave, a sluggard active, a drunkard sober, a selfish man
generous, or a cruel man kind, requires moral forces
very different from any which are to be drawn from the
philosophy of Evolution.

---

* Leslie Stephen, "Science of Ethics," p. 436.

So far as morality means simply conduct, the comparison of different systems requires time. For conduct is mainly habit; and in adopting new doctrines men often retain the habits which were formed under the old. An Agnostic will be truthful, kind, temperate, &c., from habit, though he knows no reason why he should be so; and the loss of early religious faith sometimes makes early principles of morality more precious. The type of Virtue which approves itself in the present day to minds which profess to be independent or scientific, is a type in which the features of Christ are clearly to be traced. It is Christian morality without Christian doctrine, but not without the profound influence of centuries of Christian education.

Our horizon has enlarged in proceeding from Egoism to Altruism, from Altruism to Utilitarianism, from Utilitarianism to Evolution. At each step the view sweeps over a wider area, with some loss of distinctness in detail. Egoism as a plan of life is intelligible enough, even to a child, but it is the narrowest of systems. Altruism, in its simple form of kindly affection to neighbours, embraces a widening circle, but is wanting in the range, the foresight, and adaptation of means to ends, which Utilitarianism dictates. Utilitarianism, with its well-defined practical terms, is as wide as human life, but is limited in its scope if compared with a theory of Evolution, which comprehends infinite time and space. Philosophy can form no higher aspiration than to hope for such development of intellectual and moral perceptions as might inspire an evolutionary enthusiasm, leading us to care for the order of the universe with an interest as genuine as we have in our own private happiness.

But this widening and clearing of the intellectual horizon, exhaustive as it may be, is in a certain sense blank. Open our eyes as we may to the things which are visible, we still make no advance towards the perception of things which are invisible. The transparent atmosphere, through which our vision penetrates as through vacancy, is not really void, but full of vibrations which thrill upon a duly qualified ear, though making no impression on the sense of sight. Similarly the moral universe which, from the point of view of speculative philosophy, presents no object of desire but Happiness, is to a religious mind pervaded by voices of Duty.

That mysterious power over the human conscience, the power of Divine Law,

> Which dwells not in the light alone,
> But in the darkness and the cloud,
> As over Sinai's peaks of old,

addresses a faculty in our nature distinct from the speculative or intellectual faculty, and no less essential. Reason is exercised in vain in the search for an independent explanation of the categorical "must," and the religious "ought," which are associated with the idea of Duty. One of the ablest of modern ethical treatises concludes a careful survey of the whole subject by answering "the very important question, whether ethics as a science can be constructed on an independent basis: or whether it is forced to borrow a fundamental and indispensable premiss from theology." He decides for the latter alternative, without which the Kosmos of Duty is a Chaos.*

I propose therefore in the next part to examine the moral ideas relating to Duty and Virtue which take their origin from the doctrines of the Christian Faith. In this inquiry we leave the ground of independent philosophy, but we do not leave philosophical ground altogether. Philosophy and religion move in different elements, but they are not antagonistic forces, nor are they incapable of alliance and co-operation. In short, they are no more necessarily opposed than the army and navy. The earliest of the Christian apologists, Justin Martyr, embraced Christianity as "a philosophy, the only one both sure and useful."†

---

* Sidgwick, "Methods of Ethics," p. 470. † " Dialogue with Trypho," chap viii.

PART III.—RELIGIOUS PRINCIPLES.

CHAPTER IX.

THE CHRISTIAN DOCTRINE OF DUTY.

THAT Jesus Christ is Lord of all, having rightful authority over our whole life, is the doctrine which stands as the basis of Duty in the New Testament. This doctrine is revealed as a mystery; that is, a truth beyond the range of experience or speculative philosophy, communicated by the gift of Divine Wisdom to inspired men. By the nature of the case a special revelation was necessary, to make known the eternal counsels which bore fruit in Christ's Incarnation and Atonement.

In the discourses of Christ Himself, His sovereignty is implied in the authoritative "I say unto you" of the Sermon on the Mount, in the parables of the Good Shepherd and the Vine, and in the description of the Day of Judgment, when all nations shall be gathered before the throne of the "Son of Man." These are only a few of the more obvious examples of Christ's teaching on the subject, which is altogether a clear assertion of His own Majesty in close connexion with the moral law of His Kingdom.

The same doctrine is set forth more explicitly by the Apostles, with special reference to the Passion and the Resurrection of Christ. By various figurative illustrations and similitudes, mostly drawn from the institutions of society in the period of the Roman Empire, they indicate as a first principle of Duty, that all mankind are under an infinite obligation to Christ. The mysterious dignity of His Person as the Son of God, the supernatural virtue of His Life and Death, combine to place

the whole human family in a relation of Duty to Him,
which comprehends and subordinates all particular
forms of Duty. This doctrine is one of the most
essential and characteristic parts of Apostolic teaching.
It is affirmed with more or less distinctness in the first
discourses of St. Peter at Jerusalem, in the discourses
of St. Paul at Antioch, Athens, and Ephesus, and
throughout the Epistles, being so central a doctrine of
the Christian faith that we cannot read the New Testament in any part without finding it expressed or implied.

The full exposition of the doctrine of Christ's universal
sovereignty belongs to theology. What we have at
present to consider is only the moral bearing of this
doctrine on human conduct: how far it supplies an
intelligible answer to the elementary questions, "What
is right?" and "Why must I do right?" The latter
question comes more conveniently first in order, for in
the scheme of the New Testament Duty is prior to
Virtue. The principle of moral obligation to do right
comes before the definition of Right, in the order of
Christian instruction. Among the modes in which the
authority of Christ over our conscience is set forth, six
are to be distinguished as illustrating the principle of
obligation.

1. As the Messiah, the Lord's Anointed, Christ is
invested with supreme power, as rightful King and
Judge of all men.

2. As the Incarnate Son of God, the Mediator between
God and man, He restores mankind to the family of
their Heavenly Father.

3. The effect of His Sacrifice of Himself is described
emphatically as a Redemption, that is, a purchasing of
captives from bondage.

4. The effect of the same sacrifice on the faithful is
described as Justification, that is, a release from guilt
and its penalties.

5. Under the similitude of a Body of which Christ is
Head, the condition of Christians is described as a state
of membership, begun by means of the Sacrament of

Baptism, and sustained by means of the Sacrament of the Lord's Supper.

6. Under the similitude of a Heavenly City, or New Jerusalem, the Christian Church is described as an universal society, embracing all nations, and uniting the living and the dead in fellowship through participation of the Holy Spirit.

The above six heads form a summary of the principles of Duty which were declared by the Apostles, and received by their converts. Duty is thus presented under several distinct aspects. If we proceed to inquire which of these exhibits the true principle of Christian obligation, the answer is, "One and all." The elements of moral obligation are manifold, corresponding to the elements of the moral constitution of man. Whatever lays a constraint upon our will is to some extent an obligation, whether it touch us on one or many of the various chords of our nature. Responsibility to a Divine Judge, filial reverence to a Heavenly Father, gratitude to a Redeemer, faith in a Saviour, the consciousness of a spiritual membership and citizenship, are each and all obligatory in their effects. They bind our will in a greater or less degree, according to the special form in which our conscience is developed.

The mere sense of being obliged is, so far as it goes, an obligation. If a man under mesmeric influence fancies himself unable to cross a certain line, he is kept in actual restraint by his own unreal illusion. So there is a certain kind of obligation in hope and fear, apart from the reality of what is hoped or feared; and in scruples of conscience, even though fantastic. For instance, a superstitious man will hold himself bound by an oath expressed in a particular form of words, while he breaks his word lightly in other cases. But where the sentiment of obligation is merely a sentiment, without any correlative fact, it has no reasonable ground to stand on. In this respect the Christian doctrine of Duty is distinguished from speculative theories of Duty. It rests upon a foundation which is independent of human opinion. The truth of the revelation of the

New Testament may not be more evident to our minds
than the truth of the philosophical principle of Universal
Humanity. But there is this difference : that our obligation to Christ depends, not on our assent to the Christian
doctrine, but on His actually being what Christian
doctrine declares Him to be.

For the evidences of Christian doctrine we must look
to the Old and New Testaments, and to the history of
the Christian Church. In reference to our present
subject it must suffice to assume as dogmas, given by
inspiration, the primary Articles of the Christian faith,
and only to inquire how far they satisfy the demands
of our reason and conscience, as principles of moral
conduct.

There is at least no want of obligatory force in the
principle of Duty which is laid down in the New
Testament. We have set before us a number of considerations, any one of which alone might suffice to
control our will. The difficulty is rather to observe how
the various forms of obligation are to be combined and
co-ordinated. For the principles of Christian Duty are
apt to be misrepresented, by the want of true proportion
in its various elements, as when moral obligation is
resolved into the influence of hope of reward and fear
of punishment.

If Divine Judgment were the sole foundation of
Christian Duty, there would be some reason in the
arguments of those who object to the Christian system
as leaving room for a higher morality. Filial love,
gratitude, faith, and sincere rectitude of mind are
nobler motives for well-doing than any personal calculation of gain or loss. Yet in truth these motives are
amply and abundantly illustrated in the lives of devout
Christians. It is their constant aim to serve God,

All for love, and nothing for reward.

Divine Judgment has a place in the kingdom of Christ
corresponding to that of criminal law in common life. A
good citizen does not keep the peace for fear of the
officers of justice. A tender mother, bending in rapture

over her infant, may not be aware that the law imposes a severe penalty on mothers who leave their children to perish. Her own heart dictates a measure of parental care far beyond that which the law enjoins, and it is for her a dead letter. Yet the bond of Duty subsists for her in another form of moral obligation. She feels not only a pleasure, but a sacred responsibility, in the charge of the young life committed to her arms. Similarly the law of Divine Judgment is operative only so far as voluntary motives fail to act. It is the ultimate sanction of morality, somewhat as the jail and the gallows are ultimate sanctions of human law. But neither one nor the other is the normal motive of virtuous conduct.

The ultimate sanction of Duty must needs be the Divine Will; inasmuch as Will, and Will only, is adequate to deal in the last resort with wilful disobedience. Will is also at the original source of moral law, inasmuch as our moral constitution proceeds from the Divine "fiat" by which we exist. But Christian doctrine affirms the Will of God to be a wise and beneficent Will, exercised in harmony with the highest good of His creatures. In the hypothetical case of opposition between Supreme Power and Supreme Justice, our conscience is ruled by the latter, however much we may dread the former; and the practical result will be determined by the comparative strength of the two motives. But this case is excluded by the revelation of God as Righteous and Merciful. We are often unable to reconcile the apparent course of moral government in the world with ideal righteousness; but it is a primary article of Christian faith to believe that God is of infinite wisdom and goodness, and therefore that such inconsistencies would disappear in the light of clearer knowledge.

Duty, as it is set forth in the New Testament, is a fabric built up by stages on more elementary principles, which are indicated in the Old Testament and in the history of all nations. The simplest religion of Nature ascribes to the unseen Powers of the universe some moral attributes. Observation of the course of events

shows that, in general, actions are rewarded or punished
on a plan which illustrates the moral government of
God.* Moreover, civilised life fosters the idea of an
universal Brotherhood, which finds its only logical basis
in the doctrine that mankind are children of a Heavenly
Father. These elements are combined and developed
in the revelation of Christ as the Son of God. It is not,
however, in the Christian doctrine that a connexion
between Duty and religious Faith is declared for the
first time. That connexion lies deep in the human
conscience; and the efforts of a few modern philosophers, to separate the principles of morality from the
principles of religion, are opposed to the common sentiments of mankind in all ages.

In some treatises on Christian Morals Duty is based
on the Baptismal Covenant.† This view of the subject
is not deep enough. Baptismal promises are binding,
not simply because they are promises, but because they
are promises to do what we ought. Duty to Christ, like
duty to parents, exists before we are conscious of the
relations in which we stand. It depends on no promise
for its validity, nor could any promise justify conduct in
opposition to our duty. If I promise to give to a friend
something which is my own, I am bound by that promise; but if I promise to give him something which is
his, I am bound, not so much by the promise, as by his
prior claim of right; and if I promise to give him what
is another's, I am bound to break my promise.

The binding force of a vow or promise is measured by
consideration of its nature and the circumstances
under which it is given. A promise to dispose of that
which is not our own, a promise of which we do not
understand the terms, might possibly interfere with the
discharge of our duty, and so become immoral. Sup-
posing such a promise to be made for the sake of great
private advantage, the case would not be better. When,
for example, Pope Clement V. promised the French king
Philip to do him a service, to be specified hereafter, in

---

* See Butler's "Analogy," part I, chap. iii.
† See, for instance, Sewell, "Christian Morals," chap. xvi., &c.

return for his aid in obtaining the Papacy, neither his promise nor the reward of his promise justified him in the iniquitous conduct which the King required of him.

What is wrong to do, is wrong also to promise, and therefore a promise cannot be laid down as the ultimate foundation of Duty. It is because of their inherent virtue that Baptismal vows are binding. The Covenant of Baptism is a recognition on our part of duties which are obligatory on baptized and unbaptized alike in substance; namely, to renounce what is evil, to believe what is true, to do what is right.

If the privileges rather than the promises of Baptism are laid down as the foundation of Christian Duty, this must be understood in a secondary, not a primary sense. The chivalrous rule, "noblesse oblige," may legitimately be applied to the nobility of Christian membership, as involving high obligations. Nevertheless the Law of Duty is anterior to the privilege, which is a principle of good conduct so far as it develops the consciousness of Duty, and gives fresh powers for its fulfilment. Duty originates, not in any act of human free-will, but in the eternal counsels according to which our moral constitution was formed, with relation to God and to each other. It is for man as man, as potentially a child of God, before actual adoption into the society of the children of God.

The Christian doctrine of Duty admits of no voluntary action, except within its limits. It lays down the principle that we are not our own, but subject to God in body and spirit. As redeemed by Christ, we are not at liberty to dispose of ourselves. Even virtuous conduct, if accompanied by any claim of merit, is presumption; for Duty comprises all possible virtue. The subjection of free-will to law, which was imagined in Plato's Republic, and to some extent accomplished in Sparta, belongs also to the doctrine of the New Testament, but with an essential difference. The law of express commandments is in harmony with the law of the mind within, because the Lawgiver is also the Creator. In such a Republic as Plato's, the laws of the

State would crush the freedom of individuals for want
of sympathy. But Christ's laws, rightly interpreted, are
at one with the laws of conscience, rightly informed.
Duty is not opposed to freedom, but a means to more
highly developed freedom. The truth, that to be
virtuous is to be free, was recognised by the Stoics ;
but it remained a paradox until the New Testament
unfolded the spiritual relations between God and man,
on which both virtue and freedom depend.

Consistently with this general view of Duty, the
common duties of social life are treated in the New
Testament as so many branches of duty to Christ. The
mutual duties of parents and children, masters and
servants, are enjoined as " in the Lord," that is, as incidental to the state of membership of the spiritual Body
of which Christ is the Head.*   Masters are reminded
that they have a Master in Heaven. Slaves are bidden
to do their service heartily, as to the Lord, and not to
men.†   Even conjugal duty, which might not unreason-
ably be regarded as a mutual contract, receives a higher
sanction from the analogy of the union of husband and
wife to the union of Christ and the Church.‡

A remarkable and characteristic application of the
Christian doctrine of Duty is St. Paul's method of
enjoining the duty of speaking the truth. Veracity
commends itself so obviously to the reason and conscience of intelligent men that reasons for speaking
the truth appear to be almost superfluous. Nevertheless, consistently with the general principle that all
duty has its origin in our relation to God, St. Paul
gives doctrinal reasons for veracity as a duty specially
incumbent on Christians: " Lie not one to another,
seeing that ye have put off the old man with his doings,
and have put on the new man."§   " Putting away falsehood, speak ye truth each one with his neighbour, for
we are members one of another."‖   Two reasons are
here given, distinct, yet connected together : first,
because we have entered upon a new life after the

---

* Ephes. vi., 1 ; 1 Cor. vii., 22, &c.   † Coloss. iii., 23.
‡ Ephes. v.   § Coloss. iii., 9.   ‖ Ephes. iv., 25.

likeness of Christ; secondly, because we are members of the same Body. However self-evident the virtue of truthfulness may be, these considerations place the duty upon a deeper and surer ground than the dictates of moral intuition or the utilitarian calculation of expediency.

Angry passions, sensual appetites, with all intemperance of body and mind, are denounced in the New Testament as inconsistent with a Christian character, as belonging to the old animal nature which was put off in the Sacrament of Baptism. On this ground the Apostles were able to insist, with a power unknown to philosophical moralists, on the virtues of moral purity. "Ye are not your own," "Your body is a temple of the Holy Ghost," were the arguments of St. Paul to the licentious Corinthians; and thus the sphere of Duty was enlarged beyond the limits of ancient morality. Vices which are censured but lightly, if at all, by the Epicurean or the Stoic, are reprobated as infamous by the test of the ideal standard of holiness, the "new man," regenerated after the likeness of Christ.

From the history of the early Church it appears that the principle of Duty laid down in the Apostolic Epistles was actually the rule of life of the primitive Christians. Not only within the limits of their own brotherhood, but towards their neighbours in general, they observed the laws of Christian Duty as universal laws, to a degree which is wonderful when we reflect how high a standard these enjoined. Persecution tended to narrow the range of their charity, and the reaction of subsequent prosperity lowered their moral tone, so that the primitive ideal was not sustained in the growth of the Church. Yet on the whole, judged by the evidence of facts, the Christian doctrine of Duty must be pronounced eminently adapted to human nature. It has not remained a theory on paper, like many of the grandest philosophical speculations. On the contrary, it has operated on the conscience of mankind with a power unparalleled in the history of the world.

CHAPTER X.

THE CHRISTIAN DOCTRINE OF VIRTUE.

AT the root of the Christian Doctrine concerning Virtue lies the principle, that man has no inherent power to become virtuous, or continue so. Virtue is a Divine gift, or grace, of the Holy Spirit. On this subject there is a wide divergence between the doctrine of the New Testament and philosophical systems of morality. It is generally assumed by philosophers, ancient and modern, that the knowledge and practice of Virtue are within man's natural capacity; although Socrates expressed a doubtfulness on this point, which contrasts strongly with the confidence of later speculators. To be and continue a good man, he thought, was dependent on Divine favour.* In this and in some other profound opinions he approached more nearly than any of his disciples to the doctrine of the New Testament.

How far human nature is deficient in power to act virtuously, is a question which has excited more than one great controversy in the Christian Church. But the diversity of tenets on this subject lies within a limited range; and the common faith of Christendom is in harmony with the conclusion of the Tenth Article of the Church of England: "We have no power to do good works, pleasant and acceptable to God, without the grace of God by Christ preventing us, that we may have a good will, and working with us, when we have a good will." The Latin form of this clause, "præveniente ut velimus, et cooperante dum volumus," is an echo of the language of St. Augustine, and expresses in his antithetical style the doctrine of Grace which he maintained against the followers of Pelagius.

Thus, from the point of view of Christian Doctrine, Virtue, no less than Duty, takes a theological form. While Duty is inseparable from the Doctrine of Christ's mediation between God and man, Virtue is inseparable

---

* Plato, "Protagoras," xxx.

from the doctrine of the Holy Spirit. To define and analyse the characteristics of Virtue without reference to the gifts of the Holy Spirit is a departure from the principles of the New Testament on a point which is vital to Christian morality. Christian Virtue differs from philosophical Virtue in two essential qualities which affect the general type of a virtuous character. The first thing to be noted is that Love stands supreme in the Christian scale of virtues, whereas moderation is the test of Virtue as defined by Aristotle. In the one case Virtue stands opposed to coldness of heart ; in the other it stands opposed to extremes of passion. The two standards are not irreconcilable ; but the ideas which they present are so dissimilar that a man who is brought up on Christian principles will in many respects act otherwise than if he had been brought up on philosophical principles only.

A second essential difference is the recognition of Prayer, as an element of a virtuous life. Prayer as an act of worship has not any necessary connexion with moral conduct. But prayer for spiritual light and strength is indispensable to those who are conscious of faults of nature, and wish to be made good. It might be supposed, in the abstract, that a character of this kind must needs be a weak character, compared with that of a man who firmly relies on his own virtue. Experience however proves the contrary. In some of the greatest conflicts which the world has seen, the victors have made it a point of conscience to disclaim personal merit, and ascribe their strength to the Grace of God. The Normans at Senlac, the Scots at Bannockburn, the English at Agincourt, showed no less devoutness than valour. Shakspere makes his hero say:

> Be it death proclaimed throughout our host
> To boast of this, or take that praise from God
> Which is His only.*

Belief in the virtue of prayer gave superhuman power to men like Luther and Knox ; it added force to the

---

* " Henry V.," act 4, scene 8.

arms of Cromwell and his Ironsides in battle; it gave
double energy to some of the most devoted philanthropists, such as Vincent de Paul in France, Francke
in Germany, William Wilberforce in England. Much
as self-reliance has done to uphold men under trials of
opposition and delay, reliance on Divine help has done
more.

In these respects Christian doctrine is at variance
with the chief schools of philosophy, as to the general
description of a virtuous character. But in another
important respect both systems are agreed. Virtue,
according to Aristotle, is a Habit, and this definition is
quite in harmony with the Sermon on the Mount, the
closing verses of which imply that spiritual strength is
given by practice of virtuous conduct.

The classification of Virtue in detail has never been
studied more carefully than by the schoolmen of the
Middle Ages. Living as they did in seclusion, before
the new order of society in Europe had borne fruit in
new experience and original genius, they gave their un-
divided attention to the treasures of learning, both
Christian and heathen, which had been preserved from
the past. A complete analysis of the elements of morality is given in the second division of the second part
(secunda secundæ) of the "Summa Theologica" of
Thomas Aquinas, a treatise which was the standard of
doctrine for Western Christendom during the period
which intervened between the first revival of learning
and the Reformation. It found an illustrious expositor
in Dante, whose great poem is based on its divisions;
and its influence is widely felt where the name of the
author is unknown.

Aquinas classifies virtues under seven heads: the
Three Theological Virtues of Faith, Hope, and Charity;
and the Four Cardinal Virtues of Prudence, Justice,
Fortitude, and Temperance;* personified in Dantes
vision:

> Three maidens at the right wheel in a circle
> Came onward dancing; . . . . . .
> Upon the left hand four made holiday.†

---

* "Summa," 1, 2æ, 61, 62.   † "Purgatorio," xxix. - Longfellow's Translation.

Under the head of Justice, Aquinas treats not only of rights and wrongs between neighbours, but of the offices of Religion, of Vows, and of Truth in general. Under Fortitude he includes cognate qualities, such as Magnanimity, Patience, and Perseverance. Under Temperance he includes Honesty, or Honour, which he defines after Augustine as a kind of beauty of the soul, shown in a well-proportioned behaviour, and connected with the sense of shame, which is an instinctive dread of baseness. He gives to Temperance its largest interpretation, comprising in it sobriety as opposed to gluttony, chastity as opposed to luxury, clemency as opposed to cruelty, humility as opposed to pride.

The method of Aquinas, in treating of each part of his subject, is to propound a series of questions, upon which arguments opposed to his conclusion are stated elaborately, with his general answer, followed by replies in detail. His work is encumbered with obsolete technical terms of scholastic philosophy, and by the endeavour to reconcile Holy Scripture, the Fathers, and Aristotle, as alike infallible, so that his decisions resemble judgments of a law court, where conflicting precedents are strained into apparent harmony. With similar want of critical discernment he assumes that abstract terms, such as "honestum" and "justum," have the same meaning in Cicero as in the Vulgate translation of the Bible. Nevertheless, the "Secunda Secundæ" of Aquinas is a storehouse of moral philosophy, worthy of attention for several reasons: for its comprehensive treatment of the subject as a whole, for its exhaustive elaboration of detail, and for the intellectual courage with which every difficulty is stated and encountered.

The combination of the Three Theological Virtues of the New Testament with the Four Cardinal Virtues of the Ancient Greek and Roman philosophy is the most symmetrical form in which the classification of Virtues can be presented. But this plan, having for its object the reconciliation of Jewish and Gentile wisdom, is fitter for practical instruction than for the purpose of illustrating the distinctive and characteristic features of

Christian Virtue. For these it will be convenient to
turn in the first place to the Decalogue, which sums up
the Moral Law of the Old Covenant; and secondly to
the Life of Christ, which is the standard of Virtue for
all those who call themselves by His Name.

CHAPTER XI.

THE DECALOGUE.

CHRISTIAN moralists with one accord trace in the Ten
Commandments the rudimentary principles of all
virtuous conduct. Part of the Sermon on the Mount is
a development of the moral law of the Decalogue; and
though Christ has taken for exposition only three of the
Ten Commandments, His method of interpretation is
applicable to the rest.

The Tables of Stone, on which the Commandments
were written, were the most sacred of all holy things in
the religion of the people of Israel. They were enshrined
in the Ark of the Covenant, which was itself an object
of profound veneration, and preserved in the innermost
sanctuary of the Tabernacle. Of this ordinance the
symbolic meaning is plain : that nothing on earth is so
fit to represent among men the Majesty of the Almighty
and Eternal God, as the precepts of the Moral Law.
Not the sun and moon and stars, which the Phœnicians
worshipped: not the oaks or other stately trees to which
many primitive races have ascribed mysterious sanctity:
not any image of man's handiwork, could so worthily
express the essential attributes of God as the written
words of Man's Duty.

It has been conjectured that the Commandments, as
inscribed on the Tables, were briefly expressed, without
the explanatory clauses which lengthen several of them,
especially the second, fourth, and tenth.* Some such

---

* Ewald, "Geschichte des Volkes Israel," ii., 25. Speaker's Commentary, i , 336.

theory is required to account for the discrepancy between the form of the Fourth Commandment, as given in the 5th chapter of Deuteronomy, and the more familiar form in the 20th chapter of Exodus. The latter part is given thus in Deuteronomy :—

> Remember that thou wast a servant in the land of Egypt, and that the Lord thy God brought thee out thence through a mighty hand and by a stretched out arm ; therefore the Lord thy God commanded thee to keep the Sabbath day.

These explanatory clauses, however, are of the highest importance as throwing light on the principles of the Mosaic law, and showing its applicability to mankind at large. By supplying reasons for obedience, they serve to take the Commandments out of the category of positive law into that of moral law, according to Butler's definition, " Moral precepts are precepts the reasons of which we see: positive precepts are precepts the reasons of which we do not see."* The principles which are laid down in connexion with the Commandments as to reasons for obedience, supply the ground of a religious philosophy of conduct.

The preamble is full of significance: " I am the Lord thy God, which have brought thee out of the land of Egypt, out of the house of bondage." Redemption from slavery is here set forth as a special bond of obligation to keep God's Commandments, and the same obligation, spiritually interpreted, is the characteristic basis of Christian Duty. God is revealed in this preliminary sentence under three titles: as the Almighty, as the Eternal, as the Redeemer. The first of these titles is closely related to the virtue of Faith ; the second, to the virtue of Hope ; the third, to the virtue of Charity. For God's infinite Power is an obvious ground of trust in Him ; His Eternal Being is the foundation of our hope ; and His love to us is the original source of our love to Him. In the Easter services of the Church the connexion between the Jewish and Christian ideas of Redemption is vividly illustrated, the subject of the Old

---

* " Analogy," p. 156.

Testament lessons being the deliverance of Israel from Egypt, as most appropriate to typify the effect of Christ's Resurrection.

The Commandments are negative in form, "Thou shalt not;" but when taken in connexion with God's Revelation of Himself, they imply directive laws which regulate the whole of human action, thought, and emotion.

The *First Commandment*, in excluding the worship of other gods, claims for the true God the absolute devotion of all our faculties. In contains in an undeveloped form the great precept of Deuteronomy vi., 5: "Thou shalt love the Lord thy God with all thine heart, and with all thy soul, and with all thy might." To have our objects in life dispersed is practically to have many gods, unless those various objects can be reconciled and subordinated to the love of the one Eternal God. A man's god is the supreme object of his affections, whatever that may be. There is an appearance of unanimity among moralists of different schools as to the sentiment which Pope expresses:—

> Faith, law, morals, all began,
> All end, in love of God and love of man.

But this agreement is more superficial than real; for it leaves an open question the attributes under which God is worshipped, and much depends on the choice between "Jehovah, Jove, or Lord." To some extent everyone loves the god of his worship. Mars, Venus, and Bacchus are objects of love to their worshippers. Love to God in a Christian sense involves a true conception of God's Being and Attributes according to Christian doctrine, as set forth in the New Testament, and concisely in the Apostles' Creed. It is not the love of a national or local god, still less of a god of the heathen sort, nor is it the love of a Being of unknown attributes, but the love of a Heavenly Father, who is Lord of Nature, and whose character is manifested in His Son Jesus Christ.

The *Second Commandment* forbids the worship of material images, a law distinct in its nature from the former. While the First Commandment affirms the Unity of God, the second affirms His Spirituality. The error of polytheism is different from that of idolatry, although the two are often found together. In its larger sense this commandment forbids all inordinate affections. Accordingly the Apostles condemn covetousness, lust, and gluttony, as idolatrous; and the same law is rightly understood to extend to those who "idolize or wife or child." To this commandment is annexed the sanction of punishment and reward, in the former case to the third and fourth generation, in the latter case to an indefinite number. The obligation of God's Mercy being set forth in the preface to the First Commandment, the obligation of Divine Judgment is added in the second, not as applicable to that alone, but to all.

The *Third Commandment* in its primary sense forbids perjury, and is quoted in the Sermon on the Mount in the form, "Thou shalt not forswear thyself." Its application to profane language uttered wantonly is not so much of the essence of the commandment, as the assertion of the Duty of Veracity. Consciousness of God's presence gives to all speech the sanctity of an oath, for an oath is no more than a solemn appeal to His throne. The combined influence of Christianity, reason, and experience has established the Duty of Veracity more firmly in the conscience of civilised men than any other duty, at least in England. Something is due also to national temperament. Truthfulness is the characteristic virtue of a race more distinguished for courage than for subtle intelligence:—

> Truthteller was our English Alfred named.

Northern nations have usually a severer standard of veracity than southern and oriental nations. A religious horror of falsehood is comparatively wanting in the characters which are moulded after the types of Rome or of Constantinople. Even St. Chrysostom justifies deceit in a good cause.* But the commandment stands

---

* "De Sacerdotio," i.

on a ground apart from the variable sanction of popular opinion : "The Lord will not hold him guiltless that taketh His Name in vain."

The *Fourth Commandment*, though treated by some writers as a ceremonial law, fulfils Bishop Butler's definition of a moral law, by a double title. Two separate reasons are given in the Bible for the observance of the Day of Rest. In Exodus the reason assigned for keeping the Sabbath is, in order to remember the Creation, a reason which has reference to the number Seven. In Deuteronomy the reason is, in remembrance of servitude in Egypt, which is given as a cause for releasing servants from work. Thus both Creation and Redemption are commemorated in the Day of Rest, as instituted under the Old Covenant ; and the same twofold association is not weakened, but strengthened, by the conversion of the Jewish Sabbath into a Christian festival, commemorative of the rising from the dead of our Redeemer. The consecration of one day in seven must however be regarded as a rudimentary precept, not final, but a step towards a more spiritual religious state, in which both labour and rest are dedicated to God. Similarly the words "keep holy" admit of a larger interpretation with advanced spiritual growth. Holiness means to the ignorant merely abstinence from what is forbidden ; but to the enlightened it means rather an energy of well-doing.

The *Fifth Commandment* treats of Filial Duty, which is the root of the civic virtues of Patriotism and Loyalty, with their numerous collateral branches. A promise of long life is attached to this commandment, with peculiar fitness ; for although it may be difficult in the case of individuals, to see how this promise is fulfilled, its fulfilment is manifest in the case of families and nations. A comparison of the short-lived republics of Greece, in which filial piety was rare, and the long duration of the Roman republic, in which it was conspicuous, serves to illustrate this commandment in its obvious sense. There is doubtless also a deeper meaning involved, both in the precept and the promise ;

a meaning which points to a heavenly Father and a heavenly Land.

The *Sixth Commandment* is the basis of one of the most comprehensive precepts of the Sermon on the Mount. What the letter of the law forbids is wilful murder; but the moral idea which is suggested, of all malice to a neighbour being opposed to our Duty, is developed by Christ so as to include the first impulse of angry passion in thought and speech. Offences against this and the three following commandments are punished as crimes by the laws of every state; but for this purpose the terms must be defined exactly, and the legal definition of Murder does not in all cases approve itself to a well-informed conscience. If the spirit of legislation is lax, as in countries where duelling is allowed, the law of the land is an inadequate guide as to moral guilt; and in any case moral obligation is larger than legal obligation, as we are taught by Christ in the Sermon on the Mount.

The *Seventh Commandment* is another of those on which Christ has given a commentary (St. Matt. v., 27-30). Not only the breach of the marriage law, but licentiousness and sensuality in every form, are forbidden by this commandment. The Hebrew original appears to relate to the gratification of appetite, and therefore to comprise all sorts of intemperance. As to the more judicial part of the commandment, of which the State takes cognizance, Adultery is defined by the law of the land. But if that definition be at variance with the moral teaching of the Christian Church, it is the Church, rather than the State, which has the authority over the conscience of Christians. As to the degrees within which matrimony may be contracted, as to divorce, and the re-marriage of divorced persons, the law of the conscience is not identical with the Statute law. No human legislation can be the ultimate criterion of moral purity.

The *Eighth Commandment* covers in its brief prohibition every injustice concerning property. As our social life has grown from the primitive condition of a

people whose property consisted only of raiment and
jewelry, to the complex state of the present day, in
which the law of property is the lifelong study of able
men, the significance of the command, "Thou shalt not
steal," has grown so as to forbid all kinds of fraud and
dishonesty. It is a precept of Justice in every social
relation, including for example such details as the true
return of taxes payable to the Government, and the
exercise of patronage as a trust for the public benefit.
Beyond this there is also suggested, from a Christian
point of view, the principle that all we call our own is
held in trust for God, to be administered, not for selfish
purposes, but for the welfare of our neighbours.

The *Ninth Commandment* deals with Veracity as a
social duty, in cases where falsehood is to the injury of
others. Thus Truth is the subject of two commandments, III. and IX., having reference in one case to
the impiety towards God of uttering a lie, whatever the
subject-matter ; and in the other case having reference
to the social injury inflicted by misrepresentation of a
neighbour's conduct. Political and religious controversy
abound in deplorable instances, which show that severe
moralists are apt to fail in this respect.

The *Tenth Commandment* is divided into two portions
by Roman theologians, according to a practice which
dates as far back as Augustine, in order to complete the
number Ten, after writing the First and Second in one.
But the division of the Tenth is as wrong as the con-
junction of the First and Second, for the latter part is
no more than an amplification of the former. In
Oriental language the word "house" covers all the rest,
wife, children, servants, whom it is not usual to name
particularly. At this point the Moral Law of the Old
Testament approaches that of the New ; entering into
the mental desires, governing not only actions, but
wishes, and showing that the Decalogue was given to
enjoin inward as well as outward conformity to God's
will.

While the Ten Commandments lay down for the most
part negatively the laws of human conduct, the spirit

which underlies them is expressed positively in the two great Commandments of the love of God and the love of our neighbour. Both of these are quoted by Christ from the Old Testament. (Deuteronomy vi., 4, and Leviticus xix., 18.) They are a development of the Decalogue, according to its spirit, though beyond its literal terms. In the words, "Thou shalt love the Lord thy God, with all thy heart, and with all thy mind, and with all thy soul, and with all thy strength," there is an expansiveness which has no limit. No progress in science or in civilisation can supersede this law; but on the contrary it is enlarged by every augmentation of man's resources, and by all that gives a worthier idea of God. The other Commandment also, "Thou shalt love thy neighbour as thyself," draws fresh vitality from social experience, far from becoming obsolete. Whatever is added to the stores of human happiness, in the progress of civilisation, is transferred from selfish objects to the benefit of society by means of the simple clause "as thyself."

An important distinction to be observed in comparing the precepts of Christ with the abstract theories of moral philosophy, is that Christ's laws are given for practical use, taking men as they are, with certain passions and prejudices, whereas philosophical rules treat human nature as a material to be dealt with from the beginning. The philosophical method is to survey the whole of the mental and moral constitution of man, including in some cases his physiological structure.* The Law and the Gospel deal with man as having a character partially formed, and requiring the action of guiding forces, a bridle and a spur. Even the Christian doctrine of regeneration does not imply that the primary affections and desires of human nature are extinguished, but that they are transformed by a new principle of life.

Some difficult moral rules in the New Testament are explained by reference to the character of the Jewish nation. It is evident that the precepts of humility

---

* *e.g.*, Bain and Spencer.

were addressed to a people inclined to pride and self-
esteem; that the precepts of civil obedience were
addressed to hearers who were prone to rebellion; that
the precepts concerning the Sabbath Day were addressed
to hearers who had been brought up as rigid Sabbatarians.
We might conclude from the moral teaching of the New
Testament, what is otherwise known, that the Jews were
proud, rebellious, formal, thrifty, passionate in love and
hate. In applying the same principles of virtue to a
people like the natives of South America, mild, improvi-
dent, docile, the difference of temperament must be
considered. For this reason the New Testament leaves
room for a philosophy of conduct, to add the knowledge
of human nature to the knowledge of Holy Scripture.
Practical rules of right and wrong are to be inferred
from a study of the general principles of the Moral Law,
in connexion with the particular circumstances in which
we are placed. To deduce our duty from isolated texts,
after the manner of the Puritans, would lead to falla-
cious results, often quite at variance with the spirit of
the Old and New Testaments.

Morality is progressive: for experience enables us to
define, more and more clearly, the habits of conduct
which give effect to the supreme laws of love to God
and man. Social changes give an altered form to moral
precepts, in harmony with the same original principles.
A traditional saying of Christ, which is found in one of
the most ancient MSS. of St. Luke's Gospel, illustrates
this mutability and progress. In Codex Bezæ, a manu-
script which is now at Cambridge, and was formerly in
the Monastery of St. Irenæus at Lyons, we read at St.
Luke vi., 5:—

On the same day he saw a man working on the Sabbath, and said to
him, Man, if thou knowest what thou dost, blessed art thou; but if thou
knowest not, thou art cursed and a transgressor of the law.

To pluck out the eye or cut off the hand which
offends, to offer the cheek to be smitten, to be without
anxiety for the morrow, are not measured rules of duty
addressed to men whose minds are a blank, but strong

moral curbs put upon strong passions. When we inquire calmly what is right in a given case, we must needs go back to the two maxims on which "hang all the law and the prophets." The love of God dictates that we ought to resist evil, not in our own cause, but in His: so that the precept, "resist not evil," must be interpreted with reference to the vindictiveness of human passion, not to the deliberate warfare against evil to which every Christian is dedicated. Likewise the special precepts of almsgiving are overruled by the general law of love to our neighbour; and if it be found that almsgiving tends, in certain social conditions, to make more misery than it relieves, the rule of charity under such circumstances is to refuse, rather than to give.

CHAPTER XII.

THE IMITATION OF CHRIST.

THERE still remains to be considered that which is the most vital distinction between Christian and philosophical Virtue, the influence of Christ's example. Few teachers have added anything to the intrinsic weight of their doctrine by their own personal conduct. But the example of Christ is, even more than His teaching, a law to the conscience of Christians.

No adequate explanation can be given of the immense influence which the personal character of Christ has exercised on the world, except in connexion with the doctrine of His Divinity. Human virtue, however admirable, is quite insufficient to make so deep and lasting an impression. The mass of mankind are quite incompetent to appreciate a faultless character, and they show a marked preference for strength over goodness in their favourite heroes. A Marius Aurelius is forgotten sooner than an Alexander. A Washington is not more extolled than a Nelson. If the world had seen in Christ only an Example of Virtue, His influence would never have triumphed over the religion of imperial Rome, far less retained its inexhaustible freshness. The chief characteristics of His example, "the equal balance of all excellence," "the absence of any warping, disturbing, exaggerating influence,"* are far less easily apprehended, and less popular, than the disproportionate qualities of some hero of the day, who embodies in a brilliant form the prejudices of his country or his party.

Christ's patience in suffering has taken stronger hold of the hearts of men, than all other particulars of His sinless life. What is the reason? His death, which is in some respects not unlike that of several Christian martyrs, differs from them in elements which are not merely human, but Divine: the voluntary sacrifice of Himself for the salvation of mankind, the glory from which He descended, and to which He returned as conqueror. The power which has drawn all Christendom to the Cross of Christ is the power of Divine Love, of which it is the manifestation; and the comfort of that symbol depends on the truth of the Resurrection. What the Cross represents is, not simply a crucified Friend of Man, but a risen Saviour.

Great as is the power of the moral character of Christ as an independent factor of Christian evidence, its full force can only be measured when it is taken in connexion with evidences of other kinds, such as the testimony of the Law and the Prophets. the witnesses of the Resurrection, and the gifts of the Holy Spirit manifested by the Apostles. If we contemplate the example of Christ simply in His Human aspect, as the Son of Man, we necessarily fail to do justice to the initial self-sacrifice involved in His assumption of the nature of man.†

In the "Imitation of Christ," by Thomas a Kempis, it is the supernatural virtue of this assumption of human nature, with its contingent sorrows, that is chiefly set forth as an example:—

---

* Liddon, "Elements of Religion," p. 215. † See Philippians ii., 5-11.

My Son, I descended from Heaven for thy salvation : I took upon Me thy miseries, not necessity but charity drawing me thereto : that thou thyself mightest learn patience, and bear temporal miseries without grudging.*

Christian writers for the most part have taken the same view; speaking more of Christ's humility in becoming man, than of the particulars of His example as man. Jeremy Taylor prefaces his treatise on the life of Christ, "the Great Exemplar," by a discourse on the imitation of Christ, in which he shows how the example of Christ's humility, charity, and sufferings, is infinitely magnified by the union of Divine and Human Natures in Him.†

To devout minds in all branches of the Christian Church this religious aspect of Christ's humiliation and patience is predominant. But there is a distinct moral value in the study of His life, as recorded by the Evangelists, apart from the revelation of His hidden Divinity. The critical point of view which is taken by several modern writers who, in the effort to be neutral, often contract a bias against theological prepossessions, serves in the end to set the unique power of His character in a stronger light. Of this we have a notable illustration in the following passage from "Ecce Homo :"—

It was not for his miracles, nor for the beauty of his doctrines, that Christ was worshipped. Nor was it for his winning personal character, nor for the persecutions which he endured, nor for his martyrdom. It was for the inimitable unity which all these things made when taken together. In other words, it was for this : that he, whose power and greatness as shown in his miracles were overwhelming, denied himself the use of his power, treated it as a slight thing, walked among men as though he were one of them, relieved them in distress, taught them to love each other, bore with undisturbed patience a perpetual hailstorm of calumny ; and, when his enemies grew fiercer, continued still to endure their attacks in silence, until, petrified and bewildered with astonishment, men saw him arrested and put to death with torture, refusing steadfastly to use in his own behalf the power he conceived he held for the benefit of others. It was the combination of greatness and self-sacrifice which won their hearts, the mighty powers held under a mighty control, the unspeakable condescension, the Cross of Christ.‡

---

* Chap. xviii.   † Works, vol. ii., p. 38, &c.   ‡ " Ecce Homo," p. 48.

6

Here, starting from a position independent of Christian dogma, the writer finds a profound moral significance in that twofold character of Christ's life on earth, which corresponds to the union of two natures in Him. In a later passage of the same work, the inseparable connexion of Christ's humility and majesty is illustrated further by reference to His simple assertion of His own supreme authority :—

Few, indeed, are those to whom it is given to influence future ages. Yet some men have appeared who have been as levers to uplift the earth, and roll it in another course. Homer by creating literature, Socrates by creating science, Cæsar by carrying civilisation inland from the shores of the Mediterranean, Newton by starting science upon a career of steady progress, may be said to have attained this eminence. But these men gave a single impact like that which is conceived to have first set the planets in motion : Christ claims to be a perpetual attractive power like the sun, which determines their orbit. They contributed to men some discovery and passed away : Christ's discovery is himself.*

It is only by measuring Christ's influence on mankind with that of the greatest names in history, that we can realise the fact, which stands on ground apart from all religious belief, of the transcendent magnitude of that influence. It was calmly and clearly foreseen by Himself when He said, "I am the Light of the World;" "I am the True Vine;" "I am the Good Shepherd." At the same time, almost in the same breath with these exalted claims, He bids His disciples take Him for an example; and throughout the diversities of Christian doctrine it is universally recognised, that a Christian character is one which takes Christ for a pattern.

How this can be is not obvious at first sight, because of those attributes which are peculiarly His own. But there are several suggestive sayings of Christ which go far to point the application of His example as a rule of conduct for mankind in general : "If any man would come after Me," He says, "let him deny himself, and take up his cross daily, and follow Me."†

Self-denial is the first and most intelligible of these conditions; the second, to take up the cross daily, is

---

* "Ecce Homo," p. 126.   † St. Luke ix., 23.

rather obscure. A prospective allusion to the manner
of His own death must be supposed; but also something
more. His words had probably a meaning which was
intelligible to the ears of those who heard them, before
they were fulfilled by His crucifixion. The cross, which
the Romans used as an instrument of death, was apparently formed of the stakes which the soldiers used to
carry on the march to form stockades for their entrench-
ment.* To take up the cross would thus be a significant
phrase to anyone who had seen a Roman army strike
its tents and break up its encampment. Its primary
reference would be, not to a criminal, but to a soldier, as
Virgil has described him :—

> Injusto sub fasce viam dum carpit, et hosti
> Ante exspectatum positis stat in agmine castris.†

To take up the cross daily, is a phrase which is
illustrated by this military practice, and is to be understood as suggestive of the discipline, endurance, courage,
and vigilance, which belong to the daily life of a soldier,
as well as of patience under extremity of humiliation
and suffering, which is a Christian's duty after the
example of his Master.

A similar lesson is taught under a different figure by
the act of washing the disciples' feet, of which Christ
said, "I have given you an example, that ye also should
do as I have done to you."‡ There is a solemnity in St.
John's narrative of this scene, with a careful emphasis
on the time and circumstances and manner of proceeding, by which it is raised in significance above Christ's
other actions. It expresses in a parable as much as can
be gathered up in one moment of practical Christianity.§

From these two passages a true idea might be formed
of the general character of Christ's example, although
the details remain to be filled in from study of the
Gospels. Supreme among the characteristics which are

---

* See Pearson on the Creed, p. 203, note. † "Georgics," iii., 347, 348.

‡ St. John xiii., 15. § See Jeremy Taylor's "Life of Christ," Works, vol. ii.

for the imitation of all men is that which is called Charity or Love. "Agape," the word which is used in the New Testament to denote Christian Love, is a word unknown to ancient Greek literature. Not that the Greeks were insensible to such love as manifested itself in the sacrifice of a life, the conjugal self-devotion of Alcestis, the confiding friendship of Damon. But there is a vital difference between Christian and natural affection, which requires a distinctive name. Natural affection is impatient, and easily turned to hatred; "Charity suffereth long, and is kind."* Natural affection is more or less arbitrary in its operation, being attracted by congenial qualities, by kindred, by admiration, by gratitude; Christian love has a deeper religious basis, and recognises in the alien and the wretched, and even in wrongdoers, a latent brotherhood, as children of one Heavenly Father. Compared with natural affection, Christian love is distinguished by its enduring sympathy and its unbounded expansion. Hence the principle of Love assumes a special prominence in Christian ethics.

It is in this respect that Christian Virtue differs radically from the philosophical type of Virtue. Aristotle's definition of Virtue, as consisting in the mean between two extremes,† is at variance with Christian Love, which knows no limit of too much. While Philosophy has for a maxim, "Not too much," Christianity lays stress on the opposite alternative, "Not too little," aiming always at an ideal standard beyond the reach of definition. In the one case, all emotions are put under the control of a rational judgment. In the other, judgment has a subordinate place, not restraining enthusiasm, but regulating conduct by directing enthusiasm rightly. The two principles are to some extent harmonized by union of the spirit of Love with the spirit of Wisdom. Nevertheless there remains always the essential contrast, that Wisdom is uppermost from a philosophical point of

---

* 1 Cor. xiii., 4.   † "Ethic. Nicom.," ii., 5, &c.

view, whereas Love reflects most clearly the image of Christ.

This Virtue of Love is manifested in two forms ; the one tender, sympathetic, patient, gentle, overflowing with compassion for the outcasts of society, the lepers in body and soul ; all which may be properly described as the love of Man : the other form of love being severely just and truthful, a kind of medicine or surgery to heal the spiritual disorders of the world, which is properly the love of God. As a witness to the truth, as a declared enemy of sin in every form, Christ was an example of that love which has for its object not immediate happiness, but ultimate perfection.

Love of man without love of God, if it were possible in its highest degree, would be analogous to that easy good-natured love for children which simply gives them what they ask for, and spoils their health and temper by indulgence. Love of God holds fast a high ideal of manhood and thereby dictates a moral law of Truth, Justice, and Purity, together with Charity, not as mere aids to a happy state of society on earth, but rather as conditions of Virtue according to a full development of the image of God in man, and that not for each man's self individually, but for the glory of his Heavenly Father.

Stated thus, the example of Christ is universal in its range. Self-denial, for the love of God and our neighbour, is a rule of life which the weakest can apply, while it exercises to the full the faculties of the strongest. A simple cottager can see in the imitation of Christ a rule of unselfishness, temperance, courage to speak the truth, and patience in well-doing. For a speculative philosopher the same rule points a way through the perplexities of conflicting moral principles. To follow the example of One whose conduct reflects faithfully the Divine image in His own soul, and nevertheless overflows in charity to others ; who condescends to the lowest acts of useful service, while He preaches the good news of a Kingdom of Heaven, is to reconcile the principles of Egoism and Altruism, Utilitarianism

and Evolution.   Each of these principles finds due
recognition here.   Egoism is purified of its baser
elements, when it takes the form of a desire to be transformed into the likeness of One whose chief characteristic
is Love.   Altruism finds in the Person of Christ the true
Head, in whom alone the idea of mankind as one Body
is realised.   The principle of Utility is lifted up to a
higher level by the contemplation of the life of Christ,
comprising in its beneficence the ministration of health
both to body and soul.   Finally, the principle of Evolution has in the example of Christ a clue to the future
progress of mankind, to be consummated in a new life
beyond the grave.

This view of the comprehensive range of Christ's
example is not a mere speculative opinion.   It is con-
firmed by the testimony of the hearts of men of every
race and every degree for more than eighteen centuries.
Consciously or unconsciously, all modern society is
penetrated by the moral influence of Christ.   And
while His example has been the standard of Virtue to
all Christendom, drawing all men to Him, it has exercised a power over the affections of mankind, no less
than over their conscience.   To this day Christ is the
object of personal loving affection to innumerable souls,
not seldom rising to passionate devotion.   The legend
of St. Francis, contemplating the wounds of the crucified
Saviour until, by dint of imaginative sympathy, they
left their impress on his own body, is an illustration of
the ardour of Christian love, which might serve as an
allegory, to describe how the worship of Christ passes
over into the imitation of Christ, so far as it is
sincere.

On the other hand, Christ's example commends itself
anew to those who approach it in the inquiring frame of
mind of the first disciples.   Within the last century a
spirit of free criticism has grown up, and has dared to
scrutinize with unshrinking eyes the character of Christ
as He first appeared in Galilee.   Yet the result has been
on the whole to make His example more potent in
detail than ever.   When Europe was divided, at the

period of the French Revolution, between two hostile
parties, the assailants and the defenders of Christianity,
disciples of Voltaire claimed Christ's example of
humanity as on their side. As Macaulay puts the case,
"The really efficient weapons with which the philosophers assailed the evangelical faith were borrowed from
the evangelical morality. The ethical and dogmatical
parts of the Gospel were unhappily turned against each
other."* That is, the Catholic Faith, as represented by
the Jesuits, was impugned in the name of Universal
Brotherhood, represented by Theophilanthropists and
their allies. Rousseau concludes an elaborate comparison between Christ and Socrates with the words,
"Yes: if the life and death of Socrates are those
of a sage, the life and death of Jesus are those of a
God."†

Our own intuitive discernment of the beauty of
Christ's character depends on the particular state of
moral culture to which we have severally attained. It
is a type of character which did not commend itself at
first sight to Jew or Gentile, without the aid of miraculous signs; nor is it even yet accepted without reserva-
tion by the greater number of those who profess
Christianity. So far as the imitation of Christ is the
homage of a free conscience, it is hindered still, more or
less, by the difficulty of rising to a standard so high,
even in thought. Prejudices of custom join with more
selfish motives in warping our standard of virtue. Yet
the attractive force, which is concentrated in the Cross
of Christ, draws mankind from a lower to a higher degree
of morality, in proportion as prejudices wear away.
Much that was formerly repugnant to the consciences of
Jew and Roman and Athenian in Christ's example, has
ceased to be so for us. His all-embracing love for mankind as children of a Heavenly Father, His preference
of inward to outward purity, His pity for the sickly
members of society who are cast out by the cruel animal
instinct of mankind, were once difficulties in the way of
Christian faith. Now, however, the same characteristics

---

* Essay on Ranke's "History of the Popes."   † "Emile," l. iv.

are among the most persuasive proofs of Christ's Divine mission. A large part of Christianity has been absorbed into the conscience of civilised society, as a body of self-evident truth. And it is not improbable that, when the moral intuition of mankind has attained to a higher development, new features of Virtue may be traced in the character of Christ, for which the world is not yet ripe.

John Heywood, Excelsior Steam Printing and Bookbinding Works, Hulme Hall Road, Manchester.

www.ingramcontent.com/pod-product-compliance
Lightning Source LLC
Chambersburg PA
CBHW020046030726
47499CB00007B/2609